The Murder of Anna Mae Aquash

Ruth Kanton

Published by Trellis Publishing, 2021.

THE MURDER OF ANNA MAE AQUASH

First edition. July 2, 2021.

Copyright © 2021 Ruth Kanton.

ISBN: 979-8224258918

Written by Ruth Kanton.

THE MURDER OF ANNA MAE AQUASH

RUTH KANTON

Anna Mae Pictou Aquash
Early Life

Anna Mae Pictou was born in Nova Scotia on March 27, 1945. He parents, Mary Ellen Pictou and Francis Thomas Levi, were members of the Mi'kmaq First Nation in Shubenacadie, at the Indian Brook Reserve. She was the third of four siblings, with older sisters Mary and Becky and younger brother Francis. Her parents divorced soon after, and they were left with their mother. Mary Ellen tried her best to provide for the children, but she was struggling. In 1949, she got married to Noel Sappier. Sappier was supportive, and the family thrived for a while. Anna Mae and her siblings attended the school on the reservation, and she excelled. At age eight, she contracted tuberculosis, and it was treated, but the infection had already spread to her eyes. Fortunately, she fully recovered from the infection. Sappier was a Mi'kmaq traditionalist, and he was wholly dedicated to the preservation of the Mi'kmaq culture. Through Sappier, Anna Mae was able to learn a lot about the culture of her people.

In 1956, Noel Sappier died, and the family once again had to grapple with the difficult life brought on by their abject poverty. Mary Ellen tried providing for her children the best she could, but life seemingly kept getting worse. Anna Mae was transferred to a public school off the reservation, and she found herself in the midst of a racially diverse classroom. The other students brutally tormented her, hurling racial slurs and other discriminatory insults at her. She was emotionally, psychologically, and even physically abused by some of the other students. The bullying was so bad that Anna Mae could barely keep up with her studies. The once A-student began failing her classes, and she started getting Ds in almost every subject at school. At home, there wasn't much support from her mother, who had started dating someone new. One day after school, Anna Mae and her siblings got home from school to find their mother gone. Mary Ellen had run away to marry someone else. During her time in the reservation, Anna

Mae had gained quite a lot of knowledge regarding her culture, as well as how things worked in the community. She had been working as a seasonal farmhand to help out her mother in the past, and was quite good at it. With her mother gone, she dropped out of school and started working in the potato and berry farms.

Family

In 1962, 17-year-old Anna Mae decided to leave the reservation. She and James Maloney, her boyfriend, left Nova Scotia and made their way to Boston. They found quite a number of Mi'kmaq Indians in Boston, and they settled in fairly well. The transition from living in the reservation to the city was made easier by the Mi'kmaq community, and the two became fully engrained in it. Anna Mae and James got married while living in Boston, and the two had two daughters. Denise, the first daughter, was born in 1964, and Debbie in September 1965. The two wanted their daughters to understand their Mi'kmaq roots and culture, so they often traveled to Shubenacadie.

Activism in Boston

By 1968, Anna Mae had become engrained in the Boston Native Indian society, and was participating in various programs to help with the plight of her people. She helped to set up the Boston Indian Council, attending the meetings in 1968. The council was a response to the rising populations of Natives in the city, and it was set up to help them find affordable housing. The council was later renamed the Native American Indian Center of Boston (NAICOB). Anna Mae also worked as a teacher in Bar Harbour, Maine, as part of the Teaching and Research in Bicultural Education School Project (TRIBES). The TRIBES program was set up to teach the Native Indian young ones about their history. Additionally, Anna Mae was involved with the teen program aimed at helping the teenagers to develop high self-esteem. This, she hoped, would help them to avoid the entrapment of alcohol abuse. Anna Mae had battled with alcoholism, and was hoping to help the teenagers to choose a better path. Unfortunately, the TRIBES program was shut down due to lack of funding.

Anna Mae began teaching at a daycare that was located in a predominantly African American neighborhood. She was very successful at the daycare, and she got a full scholarship to the Brandeis University in Waltham, Massachusetts. She turned down the opportunity, preferring to work with the African American and indigenous communities in Boston. At one of the meetings held at the Native American Indian Center of Boston in 1970, Anna Mae heard about the Thanksgiving Day protest that had been planned by another organization, American Indian Movement (AIM). It was around this time that NAICOB was officially launched.

On Thanksgiving Day in 1970, Anna Mae joined the members of AIM as they headed towards the Boston harbor, led by Russell Means. AIM had planned to protest during the 350th Anniversary of the *Mayflower* landing. The *Mayflower II* was docked at the harbor, and the members of AIM boarded and seized it. They were protesting the government's failure to honor the treaties made with Indian Americans, and the alleged poor treatment of Indian Americans by the government. This protest was Anna Mae's first interaction with AIM, and she decided to join them for more protests.

Around this time, Anna Mae's marriage to James Maloney was slowly disintegrating. She became aware of his infidelities, and the two decided to split ways. They got divorced a short while later.

Activism with AIM

Anna Mae's interest in activism saw her become more active within AIM, an organization that was at the forefront in fighting for the rights of Indian Americans. In 1972, the First Nations and American Indians organizations began setting up a cross-country protest, The Trail of Broken Treaties. The protest was geared towards drawing national attention to the inadequate living standards that Native Americans were subjected to, as well as the violations of the treaty agreements.

Eight organizations came together to sponsor the protest, which included members traveling from all over the country to Washington, D.C. The sponsors included the National Indian Brotherhood, a Canadian organization, American Indian Movement, National Indian Youth Council, Native Americans Rights Fund, National American Indian Council, American Indian Committee on Alcohol and Drug Abuse, National Indian Leadership Training, and National Council on Indian Work. Activists in AIM created a Twenty-Point Position paper that articulated the demands. The protesters started their journey from the west coast in October, and they got to Washington in November. The Nixon administration refused to meet with the leaders to take their position paper. In response, they occupied the Department of Interior headquarters building. The Bureau of Indian Affairs main officers were located in the same building. A number of protestors began destroying records and vandalizing the area. The stand-off lasted for a week, after which the Nixon administration met with the leaders and drew up new treaties, and conceded to some of the demand. It was during this time that Anna Mae met Nogeeshik Aquash, a native of Walpole Island in Canada. They started a relationship.

On February 28, 1973, AIM leaders went to the Pine Ridge Indian Reservation to protest the government occupation of the reservation. Russell Means and Carter Camp, AIM leaders, led about 200 protestors and occupied Wounded Knee, a town within the reservation. They were calling for the removal of Richard Wilson, the tribal chairman accused of corruption and abuse of opponents. They also protested the government's failure to fulfill the treaties made with Natives. Oglala Sioux Civil Rights Organization (OSCRO) had failed to impeach Wilson before the occupation, and later joined AIM in Wounded Knee. In response to the occupation, the government sent agents from the United States Marshall Service, the FBI, and other agencies to cordon off Wounded Knee. Anna Mae and Aquash joined in the occupation, and they were tasked with smuggling food and supplies to the residents and protestors in Wounded Knee. The occupation lasted for 71 days, and left one U.S. Marshall and two natives dead, and one protestor, Ray Robinson, missing. In the end, the occupation did not achieve the intended goal. Chief Wilson was reelected in 1974 despite the accusations against him. However, the organizations did receive public sympathy for the injustices suffered. Russell Means and Dennis Banks, AIM leaders, were later indicted on charges related to the protests. The case was dismissed by the federal court, which cited prosecutorial misconduct. Anna Mae and Aquash got married during the occupation, in a traditional ceremony presided by Lakota leader Wallace Black Elk.

After the occupation in Pine Ridge, the FBI became more determined to dismantle AIM. The activities of the AIM protestors was getting national attention, and their methods were far from peaceful, especially after the deaths of agents during the shootout in Wounded Knee. The FBI began surveillance on AIM members, recruiting informants from various chapters.

Anna Mae's marriage to Aquash did not last long, and the two separated. However, she kept the name Aquash. In 1974, she relocated to Minneapolis, where she adopted the surname Aquash. She became involved with the Red Schoolhouse Project, and worked for a culturally based school that was dedicated to the education of the American Indian students in the area. In the same year, AIM activists joined the Ojibwe activists in the armed occupation of the Anicinabe Park in Kenora, Ontario. The protests were focused on issues of police harassment, health, education, as well as other issues. In particular, they were highlighting the failure of the Office of Indian Affairs, which had apparently failed to improve the living conditions of the Ojibwe in northwest Ontario and Kenora. Anna Mae was among the AIM supporters who joined in the occupation.

In January 1975, the Menominee Warriors occupied the Alexian Brothers Novitiate in Gresham, Winsconsin. Anna Mae was part of the month-long occupation, which firmly put her in the FBI's crosshairs. The Menominee Warriors wanted the land that the abbey had occupied to return to the tribe, since it had been originally appropriated for the construction of the abbey. Since the abbey had been shut down, the tribe staked their original claim to the land left behind. The members were afraid the government would take the land. After the occupation, the FBI set its sights on Anna Mae, as she was a quickly rising the ranks within the organization. In February 1975, AIM's head of security, Douglas Durham, was expelled from AIM at a public press conference. Sometime in late 1974, the leaders of AIM had discovered that Durham was an FBI informant. The leaders had developed a sense of paranoia, especially because Durham was a high ranking member of the organization. In 1975, Anna Mae had become an important member of AIM in her own right. The organization relied on her impeccable organization skills, and she had become more involved in making decisions regarding the organization's policies and programs. Rumors began circulating within AIM claiming that Anna Mae was an informant. Instead of leaving the organization, Anna Mae began working in earnest in a bid to show the members that she was not an informant. Her need to improve the lives of other Natives drove the decision to stay, even though she could sense that the leaders were becoming increasingly hostile.

June – December 1975

In the summer of 1974, Anna Mae became intimately involved with one of the leaders of AIM, Dennis Banks. Banks was married by common law to Darlene Ka-Mook Nichols. In June of 1975, she was made aware of the relationship between her husband and Anna Mae. At the time, the organization was preparing for the convention in Farmington, New Mexico. Members Leonard Peltier, Dino Butler, and Bob Robideau later took Anna Mae to a mesa that was located in the area. Once there, they began interrogating her about her involvement as an FBI informant. She denies that she is an informant, but they keep pressuring her to confess. Once the interrogation ended, Anna Mae tells another member of AIM, Iris Thundercloud, that Peltier put a pistol in her mouth during the interrogation. When she recounted the story to her sisters and daughters, they tried to convince her to cut ties with the organization. However, Anna Mae was steadfast in her belief that the members would realize that they were wrong about her. She felt that she could do more good within the organization.

The relationship between AIM and the FBI became even more volatile on June 26, 1975. One AIM member, Joe Stuntz, and two FBI agents, Jack Coler and Ron Williams were killed. Stuntz was killed by a law enforcement officer while Coler and Williams were killed by an AIM member. The FBI began investigating AIM in earnest, looking for ways to dismantle the organization. In June 1975, Dennis Banks was on trial for his part in the Custer riots that broke out in 1973. One member of AIM, Leonard Crow Dog, asked Banks to keep Anna Mae from his farm because she was an informant. On 27th June, two AIM members, Harry David Hill and Tony Ament, bombed the Mt. Rushmore Tourist Center. The bombing put the FBI on high alert, and the leaders in AIM became even more paranoid after the arrest of Harry David Hill. The AIM leaders uncovered another informant, Bernie Morning Gun. Vernon Bellecourt, an AIM leader, appeared in Helena with Gun, and announced that informants within the organization were given 30 days of amnesty. After the time was up, he vowed that AIM would take things into their own hands. On September 5, 1975, another FBI raid saw Anna Mae arrested together with other members of AIM. She was released after 3 days, as members of AIM always bailed her out fast because of the role in raising funds for the organization. On September 13, 1975, Anna Mae was once again picked up by the FBI after she landed in Los Angeles with Nilak Butler. The two were questioned and then released.

By late October, Hill and Dog had both confronted Anna Mae about her role as an FBI informant on two separate occasions. She denied being an informant, and even joined Hill, Peltier, Nichols, and Banks in carrying out several bombings in the Pine Ridge area. The AIM leaders kept Anna Mae under constant watch, and they wouldn't let her travel to Canada. By this time, Peltier had bragged to a number of people that he had been the one who killed the two FBI agents in June. He even showed some people Coler's service weapon, claiming he had taken it from his body. Both agents had been shot from a distance, and then at close range. An informant, dubbed Informant A, supplied the FBI with the location of Peltier and Banks. Banks had gone underground before his conviction on the Custer riot case, and he was considered a fugitive. A second informant, Informant B, also told the FBI where Peltier and Banks could be found. Both informants pointed to John Chiquiti's residence in Oregon. When the FBI followed up on the information, the responding agents found themselves in a shootout with several members of AIM, including Anna Mae, Peltier, Banks, Nichols, Kenny Loud Hawk, and Russ Redner. Banks and Peltier escaped, and the rest were arrested on weapons charges. On November 24, 1975, Anna Mae was arraigned in court for the weapons charges related to the shootout that occurred ten days earlier. She was represented by Robert Riter, a court appointed attorney. Anna Mae was released on bond, and she checked into a motel in Pierre. Later that day, she was picked from the motel by Evelyn Bordeaux and Ray Hand Boy. The three traveled to Keensburg, Colorado, where Anna Mae thought she was going to meet up with Banks. On November 25, 1975, a bench warrant was issued for the arrest of Anna Mae for failing to appear in court on the September 5 weapons charges. At the time, Anna Mae was at Julian's, a bar in Keensburg. On November 28, Anna Mae left Keensburg and headed to Denver to stay with another member of AIM, Troy Lynn Yellow Wood-Williams at 4494 Pecos Street.

Murder

On February 24, 1976, Roger Amiotte, a rancher, was installing a fence when he saw a body at the bottom of a thirty-foot embankment. The land was at the northeast corner of the reservation, a few miles from Wanblee, South Dakota. The body had been revealed after the snow had melted away. The body was badly composed, curled in the fetal position, and still covered by a pair of jeans and a maroon ski jacket. The coroner, W. O Brown, conducted the autopsy. He documented that death had occurred ten days prior, and that she had died from exposure. The body was determined to be a Jane Doe. To identify the body, the hands were cut off and sent to the FBI Headquarters in Washington, D.C. for fingerprinting. A few days later, the body was buried in an unmarked grave in South Dakota as a Jane Doe.

A few hours after the burial, the FBI lab confirmed that the fingerprints from the dismembered hands belonged to Anna Mae Pictou Aquash. When the news was broken to her family back in Canada, they all refused to believe that Anna Mae had decided to take a stroll in the winter, wearing nothing but jeans and a light jacket. They insisted that Anna Mae was smarter than that, and they demanded that the body be exhumed. AIM and Anna Mae's family hired a new pathologist, Dr. Garry Peterson, to conduct a second autopsy. The pathologist from Minneapolis made a discovery. Anna Mae had been shot with a .32 caliber weapon, and the copper-jacketed bullet was found lodged in the left eye socket. He described her shooting as execution style. The bullet's entry was under the hairline of the left side at the back of her head. The bullet had then traveled upwards, but it missed the brain. Dr. Peterson also overruled Brown's estimated time of death. He concluded that Anna Mae had died approximately two months prior, and not the ten days initially recorded.

The Bureau of Indian Affairs began investigating the murder, owing to the fact that Anna Mae had been murdered on the reservation. According to various witnesses, she had last been seen in the Pine Ridge reservation sometime in December, two months before her body was discovered. The FBI also began investigating the murder, owing to the fact that they were interested in AIM's activities.

Accusations and Testimonies

The results of the second autopsy led Anna Mae's family and members of AIM to accuse the FBI of covering up the murder. Nobody believed that the first examiner was incompetent enough to miss a bullet wound, especially since Anna Mae's organs had been removed and weighed during the first autopsy. Others, including author Steve Hendricks, believed that the FBI lied when they claimed that the identification could not be done at the examiner's office. He claimed that chopping off Anna Mae's hands was completely unnecessary, and that the agents were hiding something about the case. Hendricks and a lot of other people also questioned the quick burial, done even before the FBI identified the body. Some AIM members believed that the FBI knew who was behind the murder, and that the killer may have been an informant they wanted to protect. The FBI never responded to any of the accusations brought against them.

The prosecutors working on Anna Mae's case convened a grand jury in 1976, and the details of the evidence were not disclosed. Many of the witnesses brought forward were members of AIM, and they refused to testify under oath. The grand jury did not lead to any arrests. The same thing happened in two more grand juries, which were convened in 1982 and 1994. Anna Mae's case went cold, and for years there were no witnesses or leads generated. Her family was becoming angry, especially after rumors began circulating that Anna Mae was killed by AIM. Apparently, they were convinced that Informant B was actually Anna Mae.

However, on November 3, 1999, Russell Means and Robert Pictou-Branscombe, Anna Mae's cousin, held a press conference at the Federal Building in Denver to highlight the FBI's slow progress in solving the murder. This press conference brought the case back into the limelight. Sometime in 1999, Darlene Ka-Mook Nichols, Banks' ex-wife, got a newspaper clipping in the mail. She was living in Santa Fe at the time, having left Banks and AIM behind in 1989. The clipping contained the story of Anna Mae's murder. The mail had been from her mother, who stated that there were stories within AIM that some members of AIM were actually behind the murder. Nichols immediately realized that the accusations actually made sense, and she started reaching out to her friends in Pine Ridge. When she asked about the story, all the versions had the same general course of events. She decided to go to the FBI with the information. After meeting with the FBI and agents from the Bureau of Indian Affairs several times, she was asked to wear a wire, which she willingly did.

Nichols was assigned the code name Maverick. She talked to about ten witnesses, recording several hours of conversations about Anna Mae's murder. However, many of the people she talked to were unwilling to come forward, or even testify about the murder. With the tapes, the FBI was able to get many of them to accept to take the stand, even though they were reluctantly agreeing. One of Nichols' recordings broke the case wide open. One AIM member, Arlo Looking Cloud, had just been released from a Denver prison. Over the years, Cloud had been telling friends that he had been involved in the murder. Many did not believe it since Cloud was just a low-level associate within the organization. Nichols went to pick Cloud after his release. While in the car, she started asking him about the murder, and he was more than willing to talk about it. Nichols submitted a three-hour recording of that conversation. In the recording, Cloud implicated two other AIM members in the murder. Nichols convinced him to talk to the FBI, and he accepted. He confessed to the murder, and stated that he acted together with John Boy Patton Graham and Thelda Nelson Clark.

During the fourth grand jury, the events that led up to Anna Mae's murder were finally pieced together. On December 10, 1975, Cloud, Graham, and Clark pulled up to Troy Lynn Yellow Wood-Williams' house, where Anna Mae had been staying for several weeks. They tied her to a chair in the basement, where she remained for several hours. More than a dozen people came to the house while she was tied up. Nobody tried to help her, and some even threatened to kill her. She was then loaded into Clark's red Pinto, and together with Graham and Cloud, she drove to Rapid City, South Dakota. On December 11, they took her to the Wounded Knee Legal Defense Committee offices where she was questioned by Madonna Gilbert and Lorlie DeCora-Means, in the presence of Attorney Bruce Ellison. Ellison allegedly produces a document that outlined the government's offer to Anna Mae regarding her cooperation in the shoot-out case in 1975. After the interrogation, she was taken to Thelma Rios-Conroy's home at 1014 Milwaukee St. and later she was moved to Rios-Conroy other home located on Norwood Heights. While held in the home, Anna Mae was raped and beaten. On December 12, she was moved again, this time to Richard and Cleo Gates' home located in Pass Creek, South Dakota. Clark, Cloud, and Graham then took Anna Mae, who was tied up in the back seat, to the edge of the Pine Ridge Reservation. She was marched to the grassland just off Highway 73 in South Dakota. According to Cloud, Graham then put a gun to Anna Mae's head. He pulled the trigger as Anna Mae prayed for her daughters.

On April 23, 2004, Arlo Looking Cloud was sentenced to life in prison for the murder of Anna Mae. John Boy Patton Graham received a mandatory life sentence for the murder on December 10, 2010. Prosecutors did not bring any charges against Thelda Nelson Clark because of her failing health.

Despite the arrests and convictions, many believe that the people who orchestrated the murder got away with it.

THE DISAPPEARANCE OF DIANE SUZUKI

PETER EAGLE

A hard day teaching dance. Finish work and head to the beach. It's an appealing prospect especially when that beach is the North Shore of Oahu, on the beautiful Hawaiian Islands. Whether it is standing by the ancient temple looking out to sea, having a coffee on any of the waterfront cafes or swimming in the warm blue ocean, the beach is one of those paradise-like places about which we all dream.

It might be a touch different today to what it was like back in the mid-1980s, but the ambience is little changed. On July 6th 1985, a talented and enthusiastic student planned to go to that beauty spot along with friends when she finished teaching her dance class at the Rosalie Woodson Dance Academy, located in the 'Aiea district of Honolulu.

But Diane Yayoe Suzuki never made it. Her class finished at 3.00pm, but by the time her friend arrived fifteen minutes later, the student was missing. She has never been seen since.

Diane was a girl with a bright future. She was just nineteen when she went missing; a small, petite young woman, she came in at under five feet tall and weighed just 109 lbs. She was studying at the time in the University of Hawaii at Manoa, and was already displaying a lot of promise as a journalist. Diane also had a love of dancing, and not only instructed at the Rosalie academy (to give her some pocket money during her student times), but also often performed in her academy's shows.

There was nothing in her past to suggest that Diane's disappearance was anything other than a criminal offence; she came from a loving family, and was close to her parents. Indeed, they turned up at the dance school soon after it became apparent that their daughter was not sticking to her original plans for the evening.

There, they waited in their car for her to return. It was a futile wait, although one observation they made was of interest to police. More of that later. Diane had been a success at school, and seemed happy and contented with her lot. She grew up in a comfortable home. Yes, the future seemed rosy indeed for the young lady of Japanese descent.

So little evidence was found that could be connected to her disappearance that police were struggling from the start. Her cars, keys and purse were left at the studios, suggesting that whatever happened at least began there. And that, pretty much, was that.

But where to go next? Diane's parents had observed an incident that might be of significance. While they waited in vain outside of the dance academy, feeling a growing sense of panic over their missing daughter, they observed three people leaving the centre. They were carrying a heavy trunk which they put into a car before driving away.

Costumes? Props? Lighting? Or something more sinister?

Back in the mid-1980s police had a set procedure for dealing with suspected homicides. In Diane Suzuki's case, her disappearance moved from that of a missing person to the more serious crime. Gary Dias is a retired detective, a former lieutenant with the Honolulu Police Department. He explained the problems police faced when investigating serious crime such as a suspected homicide more than thirty years ago. 'A typical homicide investigation involved interviews, diagrams and photographs. We had very little scientific work,' he explained.

But to begin with, police felt that Diane might simply be missing. They committed substantial resources to trying to locate her, and deduced in the end that the disappearance had a more worrying cause. It was six years, however, before advances in forensic testing led to police becoming convinced that the young woman had been the victim of a crime as serious as homicide. Some blood was found in the bathroom at the academy, and although it was found probably not to match Diane's (the police thought her group – A – differed from the findings), it suggested some sort of struggle. Further, testing was uncertain at best, back then, and they had no samples from Diana against which they could assess their discovery.

They decided to upgrade Diane's case from that of a missing person to one of suspected homicide.

A new chemical had found its way into their armoury – luminol. The Diane Suzuki case was one of the first in the entire country in which it was used. The luminol was sprayed into the bathroom of the upstairs studio where Diane had been working, and the blood was found.

Suddenly, her parents' observation of the trunk removed from the building carried greater weight. The shift turned from trying to find Diane, to attempting to solve her murder.

But progress was slow. Although an arrest did take place, charges were never brought.

'We did have some very good technology at the time,' recalls Dias. 'We didn't have the full understanding of all the players within the justice system about the (Diane Suzuki) case. We had lots of evidence, that we felt was evidence, and could use that to convict, more than just charge a particular person in that individual case.'

In fact, there were two main suspects linked to Diane Suzuki's disappearance. For the first, we have to head back in time to the turn of the 1980s.

Hawaii is, relatively speaking, a low crime area of the United States. As befits its Pacific status and island heritage, murders are rare. The US was undergoing a surge in violent crime during the 1970s and 1980s, however, and although the impact was felt less on the islands than elsewhere, nevertheless the period did mark an increase in violent attacks.

In the area where Diane lived, this surge of crimes hit home more than elsewhere. Eight young women – nine if Diane is included – disappeared in the space of a few years between the early and mid-1980s. A number of bodies were found, but none of the crimes were solved.

A pattern emerged between five of the murders, and police decided that these, at least, were the actions of a single person. This man, never fully identified, would become the first serial killer in the islands. Although initially police had no idea who the culprit might be, he would soon acquire a name: the Honolulu Strangler.

These five attacks all took place between 1985 and 1986, and that ties in strongly with the dates of Diane's disappearance. The strangler's first victim was Vicki Gail Purdy, the twenty-five-year-old wife of an army helicopter pilot. On May 29th 1985, a little more than a month before Diane disappeared, she left to go clubbing with friends. She never turned up. Vicki was last seen by the taxi driver who took her to a hotel at midnight to collect her car, but that was never moved from the car park.

The following morning, her body was discovered nearby; she had been raped and strangled. Vicki worked at a video rental store, one which specialised in pornographic films. Two women had been stabbed to death at the store the previous year, and for a while police wondered whether the two events were connected.

The Strangler's second victim was younger. Regina Sakamoto was just seventeen, and attended Leilehua High School. She missed her bus to school on the morning of January 14th 1986, and rang her boyfriend at 7.15 am to tell him that she would be late. She was not seen alive again.

Her body was discovered at Keehi Lagoon, the same location as Vicki, the following day. Her lower garments had been removed, and she too had been raped and strangled.

Denise Hughes was 21 years old, a secretary for a telephone company who was a keen supporter and attender of her local church. She commuted to work by bus, but did not show up on January 30th, just two weeks after Regina had been taken.

Her body was found decomposing in a stream two day's later. Her hands were bound, and she had been sexually assaulted and strangled. This time, perhaps as an attempt to disguise the body, or to make its transportation easier, the body had been wrapped in a blue tarp.

Who is to deny the possibility that somewhere in the vicinity Diane's body had been dumped? The killer had demonstrated a willingness to place bodies in or close to water. The sea around the islands are known for sharks and other predators. Could that be why Diane's body has never been found?

Louise Medeiros was the fourth person to definitely be linked to the Honolulu Strangler. Like Vicki, she was twenty-five. However, there was a slight difference in this case. Louise lived in Waipahu, but had travelled to Kauai because of the recent death of her mother. She had undertaken the journey to meet up with her extended family.

She took a late flight back to Oahu on March 26th, and arranged to take a bus from the airport to her home. Her family were aware of her plans. Witness statements prove that she disembarked from the plane and left the airport, but was not seen again.

On April 2nd some road workers made an unwanted and gruesome discovery near Waikele stream. Louis's body, semi-naked and decomposing, lay in the water. She was wearing her blouse, but was unclothed from the waist down. Her hands were, like in the cases of other victims, tied behind her back.

Another clue that was beginning to emerge in the modus operandi of the killer was the link to buses. Louise had planned to catch one – perhaps she did, but was just not identified by the driver or the few fellow passengers travelling late at night. Denise was a bus user, and had not turned up for work on the day she went missing. Had she been waiting for her commuter transport? Regina had missed her bus. Was she waiting for another?

Could this killer be picking up women from bus stops? Was that too simple? The police were, just as with Diane Suzuki, completely in the dark. But they certainly did their best. Sting operations were set up to try to lure the killer into a trap. Police women were stationed around the Honolulu International Airport and in Keehi Lagoon in a hope that they could catch the killer as he attempted to strike again.

Victim number five was Linda Pesce, a slightly older woman aged 36. She shared an apartment with a roommate, and left for work as normal on the morning of April 29th 1986. She did not return home that evening, but was expected to be late anyway because of a work meeting. Perhaps she had stayed over elsewhere. But when she did not show up for work the following morning, and her abandoned car was found parked on the side of a viaduct, she was reported as missing by her roommate.

In one of those strange twists of fate that often accompany serial and serious crimes, a 43-year-old man claimed to have been told by a psychic where to find a woman's body. It was on Sand Island, and the man took police to a specific location. The body was not found there but a search of the whole island revealed Linda's body. It was nude, and her hands had been tied behind her back.

Sand Island is a small and picturesque land mass close to the harbour at Honolulu. That is of course, the location of Keehi Lagoon.

Maybe the attacker carried out further assaults. Maybe he had previous rapes and murders to his name. But after Linda's death, the Strangler appeared to strike no more. Perhaps he became concerned at the activity of the police.

A task force had been set up from early February, after the discovery of Denise Hughes' corpse. It had twenty-seven officers, plus help from the Green River department and also the FBI.

A profile of the killer was issued. Investigators suggested that he was an opportunist, one who sought out vulnerable women. Had Linda experienced troubles with her car when she was attacked? Had the others been waiting, perhaps anxiously, at bus stops? The profile suggested he was not a man who stalked his victims. Investigators thought he most probably lived or worked in the vicinity of Keehi Lagoon, Waipahu or Sand Island.

Roadblocks were set up, and commuters stopped and questioned. Several reported seeing Linda's car near the viaduct. They described seeing a white or mixed-race man near the car, along with a light-coloured van.

Police arrested the informant who claimed to know the whereabouts of the body. It is a well understood fact that serial killers often want to stop their actions. They will sometimes expose themselves to ever greater risk in an attempt, bizarrely, to be caught.

It seemed for a while as though they had a strong suspect. The man was described by both his ex-wife and his girlfriend as being one with the gift of the gab – perhaps somebody who might smooth talk a vulnerable and afraid young woman into his vehicle, a man who could persuade a woman to take a lift with a stranger.

Both recalled his fondness for bondage; they reported that he liked to tie them up and have sex while their hands were secured behind their backs. The suspect lived in the relevant catchment area, and worked as a mechanic at an air freight carrier along Lagoon Drive. It all seemed to be adding up. Then came the news that the relationship between the man and his girlfriend was tense. They would often fight, and those conflicts sometimes occurred on the nights prior to a woman going missing.

The suspect was interrogated, and subjected to a polygraph test which he failed. But all evidence was circumstantial. The suspect was released. Following the offer of a substantial award, a woman came forward to report that she saw a man with Linda Pesce the night she went missing. She took part in a photo line-up, and picked out the suspect police had released. However, the woman feared that she had been seen by the man, and refused to act as a witness.

Could this have been the Honolulu Strangler? The evidence appears strong, but was not enough to charge the man over such wicked crimes. If this mechanic was the Strangler, perhaps the shock of such a close shave was enough to break the pattern of his actions.

Was Diane yet another victim of the Honolulu Strangler? Was there a copycat operating out there who believed his crime would simply be lumped with that of the other murdered women? Could Diane simply be one whose body was never found? If those other young women whose lives were taken were also a part of the killer's haul (and there is no certainty that they were not) then surely Diane could be another notch on his sordid belt?

Perhaps, had police ever discovered her body, they would have found tell tale signs linking her to the Strangler's modus operandi. And who is to say that killers always follow the same methods? Perhaps Diane was a victim, but something caused the killer to act differently in her case. It is surely possible that he experimented with a different way of hiding a body.

Somewhere, out there, are the remains of a young, promising dance teacher and journalist. Maybe one day they will be found and will point to a sixth or (by then, with the advancement of forensics) a seventh, eighth or ninth victim.

Or maybe not, because in the case of Diane Suzuki, another suspect featured highly on the Honolulu Police Department's horizons. The three people carrying a heavy trunk out of the dance academy on the afternoon of Diane's disappearance were later identified. They were Dewey Hamasaki, his father and his sister.

Soon evidence began to build up around Hamasaki. None of it was definitive, none was more than circumstantial, and none could be called more than tenuous. Dewey Hamasaki worked at the academy. He was present on the afternoon of Diane's final lesson there.

Yes, the trunk the Hamasaki family were carrying could have contained a body. Maybe the man had approached Diane, an altercation had taken place and some injuries occurred. Perhaps he phoned his father in a panic, who arrived, daughter in tow, to help his son remove a body.

But there are so many other possibilities regarding what could have been in the trunk.

Certainly, Hamasaki had plenty of opportunity that afternoon to attack Diane. But having opportunity certainly does not mean carrying out a deed. It is believed that the young photographer had a crush on Diane; but that is a much stronger reason for not causing harm than for inflicting hurt.

However, the police had enough, they felt, to bring in Hamasaki for questioning. They were especially suspicious regarding some scratches on his body. He claimed that he had been attacked by a rooster. The police were unsure. However, they had no evidence that was more than suggestive of his guilt, and he was released for that lack of evidence, without having been arrested.

The land around the Hamasaki family home was marshy, his father owned a pig farm. That land was searched to no avail and all went quiet until the advent of luminol and the identification of blood in the bathroom near the upstairs studio.

Police had re-opened an investigation that had never been closed but, with the passage of time, had taken an increasingly backward place in the thinking of the HPD. Now they were re-directing their efforts. They applied for search warrants to search the dance studio and the pig farm again. Initially, police were granted permission to investigate the dance studio only.

It was that dance studio where police used luminol and discovered the blood stains. It was believed that they could belong to Diane, but probably did not. Forensic skills were still developing in the early 1990s, and contamination and was a regular problem. When that blood was the last vestiges of a spillage (if it was connected to Diane's disappearance) more than five years old, then contamination risks simply exceeded the skills of the police to identify from whom it may have come.

However, the discovery was enough for the HPD to continue trying to gain the rights to investigate the pig farm, and six months after their initial request, permission was at last granted.

During the investigation, events took a turn which suggested once more that Hamasaki could be connected with Diane's disappearance. Police discovered a new looking wall, and as they became interested in the ground around it, Dewey's father became increasingly anxious, at least according to police reports.

Before a fuller investigation could occur, Keith Shigetomi, the Hamasaki's lawyer, called the police prosecutor aside, and asked him – informally – whether a plea of guilty could result in a charge of manslaughter rather than murder being pursued. But the offer was rejected, on the grounds that more evidence would be forthcoming and a case for homicide would develop.

Police searched the vicinity of the wall, but found nothing. When they tested the soil, they discovered that the wall was just six months old, it had been put up around the time that the warrant to search the pig farm had initially been rejected.

Police continued to search the property. Then, an investigator removed the stump of an old banana tree. As he dug, literally and metaphorically, into the soil he had exposed, he made a notable discovery. There, buried, were some women's clothes. They matched the items Diane had been seen wearing the day she disappeared, and they were of her size.

This, allied to the date the wall had been put up, convinced investigators that they had their man. They were convinced that the delay in acquiring the search warrant had given Hamasaki the chance to remove Diane's body, and dispose of it elsewhere. But proving their case was another matter. Although the matter was reported to the Prosecutor's office in 1991, no further action was taken at that time.

While police thought that they had enough evidence to proceed, prosecutors disagreed, and the matter rested until 1993. The then Prosecuting Attorney in Honolulu was Keith Kaneshiro. He was a friend of the Suzuki's and he believed that there was enough evidence against Hamasaki for the matter to be put before a grand jury.

'We wanted to get statements on record and under oath and called a lot of people,' he said. 'Even some who were suspects.' Among those people called before the grand jury were Dewey Hamasaki and his family. They were once more represented by their lawyer, Keith Shigetomi. This time, there was no hint of any kind of plea bargain. In fact, almost a hundred witnesses were called in total, in an attempt to make some headway,

But three grand jury sessions later, Kaneshiro admitted defeat. They prosecution team were simply too short of hard evidence. 'After evaluating what we had, it wasn't enough,' he concluded. Of course, that is not to say that Hamasaki was, in any way, responsible for the Diane's disappearance. Imagine the horror, the nightmare of living under suspicion for a crime in which you played no part. Even worse, a crime committed against a person you admired and perhaps, secretly, even loved.

Dewey Hamasaki eventually moved on, as much as he would ever be able, from the Diane Suzuki tragedy and set up his own photography business. He has published some of his work in a Christian photography book. Every time his ex-work colleague's death is raised in the media it must send daggers through his heart.

For Kaneshiro back in 1993, there was disappointment that his endeavours did not lead to an arrest, but acceptance of the fact. 'We did as much as we could with what we had,' he said. 'The difficulty of not have a body is, you can't determine cause of death. And when you have no cause, it's difficult to determine the means of death.'

Had Diane's body been discovered, hands tied behind her back, it might have been easier to understand the cause of her demise.

But that was not the case – and her body has never been found. In 1997, Diane's family eventually decided to abandon hope. They held a funeral for their missing, but loved, daughter. A year later, Diane's mother died, although her father lives on, hope fading, but not entirely gone.

Detective Lt. Dias, though, feels that it is not too late to make some headway in the case. The recent arrest of the alleged Golden State killer, Joseph De Angelo, following the combination of a chance DNA find on a genealogy website combined with advanced DNA testing has given him hope that it is still not too late to identify the killer. Who knows, that could in turn lead to the discovery of Diane's body.

Dias accepts that the processes for collecting DNA back in the late eighties and early nineties were suspect, and that contamination was a major problem. However, he also feels that this difficulty could be overcome.

'I think revisiting it (Diane Suzuki's disappearance and probably murder) would open up the thought process of the people responsible for collecting evidence and examining evidence and making decisions on the evidence. Perhaps the technology with the DNA can examine that same blood evidence and work through the decontamination processes that might have occurred over time,' he suggested.

The Honolulu police department have not closed Diane's case, and they too remain open to future developments. '...homicide detectives stepped up their efforts to review unsolved murder cases,' said a spokesman in a statement to the news media. 'The continue to look for untested evidence and any evidence that should be retested using updated DNA technology.'

While they would not comment specifically on Diane's situation, because her case remains open, they pointed out that no statute of limitations exists where homicide is involved, and therefore any future findings will be properly investigated. 'We are committed to getting justice for victims and their families, no matter how long it takes,' the statement concluded.

In 2014, updated DNA testing procedures led to the conviction of Gerald Austin, who was convicted of murdering an 81-year-old Hawaiian woman, Edith Skinner, in 1989. Whether the same fortune will smile upon that young girl with such a promising life in front of her remains to be seen.

Diane Suzuki ended that dance lesson at the Rosalie Woodson Dance Academy back in the summer of 1985 expecting to enjoy a lively evening of fun with her friends. Whether we will ever know what happened to her is something about which we can only hope.

KILLER MISTRESS: THE TRUE STORY OF TANIA HERMAN

28

LINDA CARLISLE

Tania Lee-Anne Herman, better known in the Australian media as the body-in-the-boot or Mum-in-the-boot killer, was born in Rochester in 1996, just south of the city of Echuca. Echuca is a small town located on the banks of the Murray River and the Campaspe River in Victoria, with its name meaning "Meeting of the Waters" in the local Aboriginal dialect. The town has a population of just over 13 000 and is known as the paddle steamer capital of Australia. Tania was born into a simple, country family. She was the youngest of four children, and she enjoyed a safe and inspiring childhood. Tania was a promising junior swimmer, having won several titles at the state level, and had an incredible flair for the arts. Her lawyer, Julie Sutherland, commented later in her life that Tania "was the embodiment and quintessence of everything noble and decent which one comes to equate with country living, including a strong work ethic and getting on with life despite its vicissitudes." As a high school student, she made money on the side by creating floral bridal hairpieces. None of her friends or family members would have said that Tania was suffering from any difficulties in her younger life, from an early age Tania learned to hide things that were causing her grief. This became something that was characteristic of her throughout her life in an attempt to not cause concern for others.

Before she met "soul mate" Joe Korp who would eventually manipulate Tania into actions that would deprive her of twelve years of freedom, Tania had three significant relationships that left her in a damaged and compromised position. She also endured years of sexual abuse as a child, which she was told was "a special kind of love". When she was older, Tania's first marriage was to John Linton on Sep 26th, 1987 when she was just seventeen. Linton was older than Tania, and their relationship only lasted five months. After this time, Tania met a Columbian student when she was twenty-one and they had a two-year romance. During this time, Tania had her first child, but her partner was cheating on her and Herman eventually found out about the other woman. Her boyfriend left, and later married the woman that he was cheating on Tania with. Finally, in 1996, Tania married Paul Herman who was a charter boat operator in Queensland. Things seemed that they might start to become more stable for Herman. They had Tania's second daughter and moved back to Echuca. However, her husband was a big drinker. Tania reported that her husband would at least go through several slabs and a bottle of bourbon each week and that this began to concern her. However, the real issue for Tania was when Paul became physically violent towards the end of their relationship. In Tania's opinion, this behavior was fueled by his dependency on alcohol and she didn't see a future for them if this continued. Tania left Paul in 2002.

When Tania was 30, she was diagnosed with cervical cancer and had to undergo chemotherapy and radiation therapy for six months. Tania decided not to tell her family about her health issues. When she lost her hair, she claimed that she had shaved it for charity. Tania's desire to keep the troubling news to herself might have made it easier for the manipulative man who was about to arrive on the scene and ask more of Tania than she ever believed she would be capable of doing. After a string of unsuccessful relationships and marriages, Tania, a vulnerable single mother of two, went in search of a new partner online. Unfortunately for her, she stumbled across Joe Korp.

Joe Korp, who was registered on the dating site as Joe Bonte, was posing as a single, self-employed builder. The factory worker was married to Maria Korp, a woman who had immigrated to Australia from Portugal with an earlier, failed marriage. Maria helped to build their house in North Melbourne, being the project bricklayer on the house and directly involved in much of its construction. Unfortunately, almost immediately after they moved in both partners began to express unhappiness in their marriage. Maria had a daughter, Laura, from a previous marriage, and she and Joe had their son Damien together early on in their marriage. When Joe initially connected with Tania in a chat room in October of 2003, he kept his marriage to Maria a secret. There are conflicting claims from different prosecutors as to when Tania became aware of the marriage, some claiming early on and others maintaining that Tania wasn't aware for up to 12 months into their relationship. Whether Tania found out about Maria earlier or later is not of great concern, as this information did nothing to deter her from meeting up with Joe and planning their future life together. During this time, Joe was also seeking out other relationships online, but he provided Tania with a sense of security that he had been searching for her for his whole life. Sources did not report whether or not be actually met up with other women, but the frequency with which he was away from home and the number of times that he was visiting Tania suggest that he had several women. This period may have even been a test for several of these women as to who Joe determined would be capable of killing in the name of their love for him.

The first time that Joe drove to Echuca to meet Tania in February 2004, she showed him the sights around town before having sex in his car down by the Murray River. Joe made many trips like this one over the coming months, hiring cars for the drive and telling Maria that he was in Sydney on business. Joe began to promise Tania the world, even going as far to say that he wanted to buy wedding rings together and have a ceremony in her house as a sort of temporary marriage until they were able to have a real one. Joe promised children to Tania, a long life together, and her much-craved stability. From the moment that she met Joe, Tania began to act as if she was under a spell. Even Tania's lease was registered under the name of Tania Herman Korp. When Paul Herman, one of Tania's previous husbands, had a heart attack while working on a paddleboat, Joe attended the funeral with her. Paul's family later remembered his face when Maria's case was all over the television and newspapers, and some have even wondered whether Pau's death might have occurred under suspicious circumstances. When Joe spoke to Tania, he described his then present marriage as unhappy and sexless, telling Tania how much he was looking forward to the life that they could share together when he was no longer with Maria. Joe assured Tania that the only reason that he hadn't already left Maria was that Maria held incriminating evidence against him and had threatened to take this information to the police if he ever left her. Joe never specified what this information was, holding a lot of things back from Tania. Herman, however, couldn't see this approach.

At this time, Joe became manipulative and domineering. Joe told Tania that he preferred her to only wear black, so those were the clothes that she donned. He told her to distance herself from her friends, so she became isolated. In a prison interview after the death of Maria Korp, Tania divulged information about her mindset at the time. "I think I was sort of brainwashed by him because I was so in love with him and he used to promise me the world — that we'd be married and we'd have a house and we'd have a family and ... it's just one thing after another," she claimed. Eventually, Joe even went so far as to ask her to move closer to him. Tania sold her house and moved to Greendale, by this time acutely aware of Maria and Joe's children. All this time, Joe was finding and meeting up with other women online just as he had done with Tania, but she was unaware of this fact. It is also likely that Joe began to see more of Tania at this time due to her closer location, and that this led to Maria confirming her suspicions that her husband had a mistress. Little did Maria know that events were falling into place that would eventually result in her assault, attempted murder, and death.

In Greendale, Tania enrolled her youngest daughter at the same school as Joe and Maira's son Damien. She even went so far as to list Joe as the emergency contact for her child at the school's office. By this time, Maria was aware that Joe was having an affair. One day, Joe came home to the locks changed and all of his belongings on the lawn. Maria had told friends and relatives about the weekends she spent alone as Joe was on his 'business trips'. During this time, Joe moved in with Tania and he met members of her family, including her brother Stephen Deegan. However, after a brief period, Joe returned to Maria on Christmas Eve. He phoned Tania to assure her that there was still hope for them together, and this is when the pair first began to plot the death of Maria Korp. Tania has stated that the plans began up to a year before the day that she waited for Maria in her garage. During this year, there were a variety of plans including staging a burglary where Joe could bash her to death, and running over Maria with a car. Joe even looked into the cost of hiring a hit man. However, in the end, they settled on Tania taking Maria's life, or what Joe always referred to as "taking care" of his wife, or "getting her out of the road." As the two continued to discuss these ideas, they moved away from a fantasy where they might be able to live together and closer towards practical actions. It is difficult to say whether Joe genuinely wanted to live with Tania and have a future with her. Perhaps if there had been less of an investigation into the matter and he didn't feel the need to incriminate Tania there would have been room for such a life. Either way, at this point, Tanis had no doubts that everything that they were planning was for the future of their love.

During Joe Korps's stay at Tania's house, they discussed how to kill Maria at a pre-Christmas barbecue where her brother Stephen was present. Stephen later contacted the police on the 14th of February regarding the disappearance of Maria Korp, stating that his sister and Joe had talked about several ways of killing Maria in front of Stephen, including using a belt as a ligature. They also asked for Stephen's opinion, saying "What's the best way to knock someone off?" Stephen said that he had encouraged his sister to break off all contact with Joe, and that he "Was crazy and that she should get rid of this guy". As he told police about her reluctance to stop seeing Joe, he noted that it was "Like he had brainwashed her." Stephen also mentioned that in late January Joe was present again and that he and Tania spoke freely in front of Stephen about killing Maria. Furthermore, the night before Maria's disappearance, Tania called Stephen and asked that he visit her as she had something to discuss. During this phone call, Tanis was considerably distressed and going through a moral dilemma. The following is Stephen's account of that discussion as he stated it to the police:

"Tania told me that she and Jo were going to kill Maria. She was very matter of fact about it, and it was like she had already done it. She told me that she was going to use thin cotton gloves, dye her hair, use a swimming cap and black beanie over the top. She also told me what clothes she was going to wear. She said that Jo was going to pick her up and take her to his place. On the way, they would stop and she would get into the boot so that he could smuggle her in. Then she was going to hide behind his car and wait for Maria. She would then sneak up behind her and try to strangle her with a belt. After this, she would put her in the boot of the car and drive the car to the Shrine in Melbourne."

On the morning of the 9th February 2005, Joe Korp drove Tania to his Mount Ridley address at around 6:00AM where she was to lay wait in the garage until Maria came down to drive to work. Joe and Tania had a short conversation in the garage, where he assured her that he loved her. Tania later recounted to police that Joe asked her "How much do you love me? Are you going to show me today?" and also told her that she must make sure that Maria doesn't leave the garage alive. "You've got to get rid of her for me. I want her strangled. I want her dead." Tania had dyed her hair and was wearing the swimming cap, gloves, and black beanie, just as she had told Stephen she would. She hid behind Laura's car and began to rationalize what she was about to do. As she sat there with the strap, and remembers thinking "I shouldn't be doing this. It's not right." Joe had already left for work and the only thing that allowed her to continue the act was repeating Joe's words over and over in her head again that she mustn't let Maria out of the garage alive. In this way, she became somewhat distanced from her actions and it allowed her to go through with the tasks that lay ahead.

When Maria came down the stairs, Tania hooked the strap over Maria's neck and began to apply pressure. Maria screamed and they both tumbled to the ground, Maria fighting for her life and Tania fighting for love. Tania, being physically stronger and larger than Maria, was able to overpower her and won the struggle through sheer force. During these moments, Tania continued to ethically struggle with the actions that saw she herself committing, later saying that "I was in a set frame of mind, but as soon as I saw the blood, something snapped. I panicked," she says. But yet again, by keeping Joe's words in her mind she was able to get through the ordeal. Eventually, Maria slumped down onto the ground and stopped moving. Tania picked her up and dumped Maria in the boot of her own car before taking the keys and preparing to drive to the Shrine of Remembrance in Melbourne. "As I was driving, I couldn't stop crying. I kept thinking, 'This is wrong, this is wrong," Tania claims. On the way, Tania would hear Maria breathing in the boot and came to the realization that she wasn't dead. She heard other sounds as she drove, but didn't know what she could do about the situation. When she got out of the car, the considered other actions that she might take, but settled on leaving Maria in the boot to die. This added another layer to Tania's ethical dilemma, as the death had not been clean cut. For days she would be forced to think about the fact that the woman was still alive in the car, and that every moment that she wasn't going back to retrieve her she was condemning her to death. The only thing that brought her any clarity at this time was the knowledge that now the hardest part was done, and that if they were able to get through the police investigation she and Joe would be able to start the new life that they had spoken so much about. However, Tania was soon to find out that Joe would betray her in his interviews where he would name her as the likely killer.

After parking Maria's car at the Shrine of Remembrance, Tania rushed to Stephen's work on Elizabeth Street in Melbourne at 8:30AM. She asked her brother to drive her to her home in Greenville and seemed calm and collected. Tania told Stephen that she had done as she claimed she would, and killed Maria Korp. Stephen had not previously contacted the police as he didn't believe that his sister would be truly capable of these crimes. Even when she arrived at his workplace and openly confessed, he still didn't believe she had truly done it and took this as one more step to mislead him. Stephen was extremely worried for his sister, and would make fresh attempts to encourage her not to be in contact with Joe, but he was certain that the events that Tania was claiming had passed were either figments of her imagination or attempts at some guise. It wasn't until he saw the news coverage when Maria was found in the boot four days later that he accepted his sister's crimes and called the police to fill in as many details as he could. Tania then met up with Joe and gave over the keys to Maria's car. She told Joe that she was concerned that she hadn't successfully killed Maria, and so that he was "taking a life." Joe allegedly replied: "No, you took the life for me," and soothed Tania, maintaining that she would not be caught. Joe told her to go out into the Lake Eppalock area and burn all of the items that implicated them in the crime. These items included not only the gloves, beanie, swimming cap, and belt that Tania had used at the scene, but also a number of other things that the couple has used as they planned the assault. Other items were also later buried at the Greenvale Reservoir. Later that evening, Joe Korp reported Maria as missing to the Craigieburn Police.

When Joe was interviewed the next morning, the police discussed his relationship with his wife, their financial position, their working commitments, and Joe's connection with Tania Herman. During this interview, Joe was asked if he could think of anybody that would want to hurt Maria, and he immediately told the police that he believed Tania had done it. Joe claimed that Tania wished ill will of Maria and that she was jealous of their marriage. He denied any involvement in the disappearance of his wife, and Joe also claimed that he was slowing down the relationship with Tania. The police then interviewed Herman, who was described as being very cooperative with the police but maintained not only that she hadn't been involved with the crime, but that she had never met Maria and didn't know her. When Tania was released on this day, she attempted to make contact with Joe. She tried to connect with him twenty times through calls and messages, but he didn't respond to any of them. It was around this time that Tania started to wonder whether Joe was planning this all along, and had used her to get out of his marriage with Maria safely and without allegations regarding the sensitive material that his wife had claimed she held. She now began to feel that she had been thrown under the bus, doing Joe's dirty work for him and bound to get stuck with the consequences.

The search for Maria Korp continued for four long days until a gardener recognized her car from the news bulletins. Those who opened the boot claim that they thought Maria was already dead due to the stench and the state of her body. When they realized that she was breathing, Maria was rushed to the Alfred Hospital and put into intensive care. The initial diagnosis was that she had suffered from strangulation, dehydration, and prolonged loss of consciousness, which had resulted in brain injury. Later on that day, Maria was examined by Forensic Physician Dr. Morris Odell, who categorized which injuries were a result of the initial struggle and which were a result of her incarceration in the boot of the car. Odell noted that her neck injuries were likely caused by the application of a ligature. Maria stayed in a coma, and she was fed intravenously before being moved onto nasogastric feeding before percutaneous entrogastric tube feeding. The doctors monitored her neurological state with MRIs, which showed a progressive loss of brain substance which suggested that her initial diagnosis of having a severe hypoxic brain injury was accurate. When Maria did not improve over months, the decision was made on the 27th July to cease her medical management and tube feeding as her condition was perceived to be terminal. At fifty years old, Maria Korp died in Alfred Hospital at 2:40AM on the 5th August 2005.

On the afternoon of the 16th February 2005, both Joe and Tania were interviewed once more. For the third time, Joe was interviewed and maintained his stance that he had nothing to do with the attempted murder of his wife. Joe made no comment on the questions that were asked of him, and Tania Herman made full admissions to not only her involvement in the attempted murder but details about Joe being her accomplice. By this time, Tania had realized Joe's intentions to pin the entire event on her and had begun to wake up from her spellbound period of infatuation with him. Even though she still loved Joe dearly, she felt that the truth about the situation had to be told. Tanis was charged with attempted murder. On the 1st July 2005, Tania was charged with twelve years imprisonment with a non-parole time of nine years. Joe Korp, who was charged and remanded in custody, had been released on the 9th June to stand before the Supreme Court on the 3rd August. Joe wrote a letter to Tania, which he had his sister deliver. In this, he insisted that there was still a chance for them if she wanted it. "I think I was sort of brainwashed by him because I was so in love with him and he used to promise me the world — that we'd be married and we'd have a house and we'd have a family and … it's just one thing after another," Tania claimed. Over the years to come, through the counseling that she would receive in the prison system and the friends that she would make there, Tania would come to understand that way that Joe treated her. These new perspectives would give her a whole new outlook on these years of her life and the ways in which he was treating her.

On the day of Maria's funeral, Joe went out into the shed of the house that he shared with Maria. He wrote a series of diary entries, notes, and letters, and stuck up pictures of Maria on the shed walls. Joe hung himself, and one of the notes which were left close to where he was found hanging read "F-ck all those who thought I was guilty" and "Where's the justice...no f———evidence." In all of these letters and diary entries, he maintained his innocence and his love for Maria. In one letter to a daughter of his, Mia, from a previous marriage, he wrote:

"Mia, Oh my only daughter.

"I have loved you and cried for you all my life.

"It was nice to see you and become close again.

"Please forgive me for leaving you again.

"Please understand about love.

"I found it and lost it with Maria.

"Stupid me."

At this time, Herman was devastated. In one session with the prison counselor, she revealed: "If he's not alive I don't want to live." Tania went into a long period of silence after this, resistant to talking about the case with anybody who came by to interview her. Eventually, she opened up to one writer, Rochelle Jackson, who was putting together a collection called Partners in Crime: The true stories of eight women and their lives with notorious men which were published in 2012 by Allen and Unwin. It is from these interviews that we have come to understand so much more about Tania and the experiences that she went through. It is also due to this text that we can gain some insight into how she was reflecting on her actions and her time with Joe. During this interview, Tania expressed to the world that her biggest regret was taking a mother away from her children, eleven-year-old Damien and twenty-seven year old Laura. Tania, a mother herself, found herself haunted by this fact and named this as the place where she harbored the most guilt regarding the whole series of events. Tania only had sporadic contact with her own daughters during her jail sentence. Eventually, Tania began to show signs of accepting the things that she had done and wanting to grow past them: "I've done his crime and now I'm doing his time. The past is the past and I can't undo it — I just have to move on."

Tania was initially incarcerated in the Dame Phyllis Frost maximum security prison. It is Victoria's largest women's prison, holding 260 prisoners, and dedicated to the philanthropist Dame Phyllis Frost, who was particularly concerned with the welfare of female prisoners. Aside from Prison Tarrengower which is a minimum security prison, which Tania was later transferred to, The Dame Phyllis Frost Centre is the only women's prison in Victoria. Aside from Tania Herman, there are several other prisoners who have spent time at the center that have captured Australian headlines. Vicky Roach, an indigenous activist, fought the

High Court while in jail in a case that overturned an attempt to remove the vote from serving prisoners. Andrea Mohr, a German writer, served time for international drug smuggling and organized crime. Wendy Peirce, Roberta Williams, and Renate Mokbel were also inmates of the facility, both being figures in the Melbourne underworld as represented in the popular Underbelly series. However, probably the most famous inmate is Judy Moran who was the queen of the Melbourne underworld, murdering her brother-in-law Des "Tuppence" Moran. There are rumors that Herman and Moran had an altercation one day in the prison, but these allegations were denied by prison staff. The claim was that Herman had won a turf-war in the prison, with Moran having previously been the top dog. In the center, Herman was known as Muscles. Some sources claim that Tania punched Moran, and others claim that this turf-war was won purely on words. Tania was eventually moved from the maximum security prison to Tarrengower, where she began to pick up the pieces of her life.

Tarrengower held a lot of opportunities for Tania. During this time she began a degree in fine arts, took an interest in cooking, dressed up as Santa for the Christmas celebrations, and developed a friendship with her cellmate Bernadette Denny. Denny was in the system for the Herman Rockefeller murder which had occurred in January of 2010. Denny, an alcoholic pensioner, and her partner Mario Schembri, a sheet metal worker, got into contact with millionaire Rockefeller through an advertisement for couple swinging in a local newspaper. Herman claimed that he and his wife were interested in swinging together, but when he arrived he was alone, his wife knew nothing of the matter. Herman engaged in intercourse with Denny while Schembri watched, and promised to bring his wife the next time that he arrived. When he arrived frazzled one evening demanding sex of Denny with no wife in sight, the couple became aggressive. Rockefeller kept attempting to grab and sexually assault Denny, So Schembri and Rockefeller became involved in a brawl which Denny joined. This interaction became more and more violent until Rockefeller apparently fell over and knocked his dead, causing his death. After this, the couple went shopping for materials to dispose of the body, being seen on a hardware store camera buying plastic drop sheets and testing the weight of a chainsaw. They dismembered his body and Schembri took the remains to a friend's house where he burnt the parts over time. Tania became very close to Denny, and publically defended her as a good woman. During this time, Tania also met her current lover Nicky Muscat.

Nicky Muscat was in Tarrengower as a fraudster, having stolen $118 000 from the pokies venue that he had managed. During their time at Tarrengower, a relationship developed between Nicky and Tania and they even asked for a ceremony where they could be married behind bars. This event became highly publicized in the Australian media and brought a lot of attention back to the case. This request was denied, but their love stayed strong. On the 14th February

2014, Tania Herman was released from prison. Nicky, who had been released from the prison the year earlier, arrived to pick her up in a silver 4WD and took her to her home in Yarraville. Over the next few days, the couple was spotted walking around their local streets and stores hand-in-hand, with Tania beginning to pick up the pieces. Tania and Nicky are still together, adjusting to life on the outside and trying to make up for the time that they each lost in prison. Perhaps they offer each other an understanding that many people would not be capable of. Finally, Tania has found a relationship with the stability, respect, and understanding that she has always been looking for.

KILLER GRANNIES : TRUE STORIES OF SERIAL KILLING SENIORS

ERICA BYRAM

Dorothea Puente became infamous in the 1980s for being the "Death House Landlady". She ran a boarding home in Sacramento, California and proceeded to steal the Social Security checks of her elderly and mentally disabled tenants. Those tenants who proved to be too troublesome would be given increased dosages of sleeping pills until they died. She would chop up the bodies and bury them in her backyard.

EARLY LIFE

Dorothea Puente was born Dorothea Gray on January 9th, 1929 in Redlands, California. Both her mother, Trudy Mae, and her father Jesse James Gray, worked as cotton pickers in Central California. Her father would die of tuberculosis in 1937 while her mother would die the following year in a car accident.

Dorothea was delusional so some parts of her childhood have conflicting accounts. She states that she was the product of two alcoholic parents and that her mother was working as a prostitute before she died. She claimed her father was mentally unstable and often threatened to kill himself with a gun pointed to his head in front of the children (Dorothea would sometimes claim to be one of fourteen children.)

What is clear is that she was orphaned at the age of nine. Dorothea would then live in different orphanages, claiming to be sexually abused at one in particular. Eventually, her relatives from Fresno took her in. In her later years, she would discount the fourteen children claim and state that she was one of three children who were all born and raised in Mexico.

Dorothea would marry at the age of sixteen to a returning soldier named Fred McFaul. She would have two daughters a year later. Dorothea would give up both daughters, sending one to relatives in Sacramento and the other for adoption.

Dorothea would suffer a miscarriage in 1948 and McFaul would divorce her that same year. Angry at the failure of her marriage, she lied to everyone about the divorce and said that McFaul died of a heart attack shortly after their marriage ceremony.

She then turned to a life of crime. She would steal and forge checks. Dorothea would be caught in a forgery scam, serving six months of a one-year sentence. She would meet another man and become pregnant again. Dorothea would put the baby up for adoption as she hardly knew the man and could not afford the baby.

In 1952, she would marry a Swedish man named Axel Johansson.

CHOOSING A LIFE OF CRIME

Dorothea Puente would be married a total of four times with two documented divorces. She had another daughter which was put up for adoption at birth. The two would eventually meet, however, in 1986. Her daughter would describe her birth mother in unflattering terms, saying that she had "no real personality."

Dorothea would divorce Johansson in 1966 and marry Roberto Puente, a man that was almost twenty years her junior. The union would last only two years but Dorothea would keep his last name.

"Interesting that Dorothea would keep the last name of Puente," forensic psychologist Paula Orange said. "It became part of her con. She used the Spanish surname to con people into thinking that she was of Spanish descent. It helped her get some clients later on as she would use her surname as some kind of ethnic connection with them as in the case of the Costa Rican Bert Montalvo. She also cultivated a harmless old lady exterior in order to get people to put their guard down. She would tell people that she was seventy when in fact she was only fifty-nine. This con, this illusion would aid in her avoiding detection from social workers, parole agents and even the police."

Married life did not deter Dorothea's penchant for crime. Moving on from check forgery, she would run a brothel before being caught and arrested in 1960. Her sentence was relatively light, serving 90 days before being arrested for vagrancy and serving another three months.

Putting on a veneer that she was rehabilitated, Dorothea began working as a nurse's aide, providing care for physically disabled people and senior citizens in their private residences. This experience put a an idea in Dorothea's head.

She would manage boarding houses and cater to the elderly.

Dorothea finagled her way into becoming a manager for a three-story, 16-bedroom care home in Sacramento. She would marry for a fourth time, to a "raging drunk" named Pedro Montalvo. The union would only last a few months as Dorothea now took to trolling bars looking for older men who were receiving Social Security. She had the ability to put together tall tales, most often that she was a "famous actress" and told these men of her movie roles in films that didn't exist. In these movies, she always played the "evil woman." She also promoted herself as a "holistic doctor" and would listen intently to the maladies of her disabled mark before offering a suggestion on how they could improve their health. These stories would always lead to her convincing her mark to become one of her tenants after which she would steal their government check. She would talk a few into becoming her tenants the she would steal their government checks.

ARRESTS AND MORE ARRESTS

In 1982, Puente would be arrested for drugging and robbing people she would meet in bars. She would serve two and a half years in jail before she returned to her boarding house duties.

"Dorothea struck everyone as a harmless figure," Orange said. "So when she started the boarding house no one in their right mind would see her as a threat. They saw her as a sweet old lady. Her boarding house was spotless, inside and out. You could take a white glove, run your fingers across the furniture and not come up with a speck of dust."

Puente was a meticulous gardener and neighbors would describe her as being "very protective of her lawn."

"If somebody walked on her lawn," a neighbor said. "She'd cuss them in language that would make a sailor blush."

It would be this same year that the murders began. Dorothea had a friend named Ruth Monroe who began living with her but would die shortly after from a pharmaceutical drug overdose.

"She was sad," Puente told police when they came to investigate. "Very sad. Her husband was dying."

The police believed her and the death was ruled as a suicide.

"This is the occasion where Puente learned how to game the system," Orange said. "She learned that if there was no crime scene there was no crime. The police found Ruth Monroe dead and really had no choice but to declare it a suicide as there was no evidence that a murder had taken place. That was probably the farthest thing from the mind of the police. How could this sweet old lady be guilty of drugging up her best friend then smothering her with a pillow. She just didn't fit the profile."

Only a few weeks later, the police would return as a tenant named Malcom McKenzie would claim that Puente was drugging and taking money from him. Puente would be investigated and charged with theft. Sentenced to prison for five years, she began a pen-pal correspondence with a man named Everson Gillmouth, a 77-year-old retiree living in Oregon. Puente was then released after serving only three years of her sentence and found the smitten Gillmouth waiting for her.

They soon began making wedding plans, Gillmouth quickly opening a joint back account as they moved into an apartment in Sacramento together.

In November of 1985, Puente would hire a handyman named Ismael Florez to install some wood paneling in her apartment. She paid the handyman and threw in Gillmouth's 1980 Ford pickup as part of the payment.

"My boyfriend no longer needs it," Puente said. "I'm also wondering if you could build me a box. Say six feet by three feet by two feet. Just need to store some books and stuff."

Florez agreed and Puente would fill the box with her "stuff". She then hired Florez to help ship the nailed-shut box to a nearby storage depot. Puente accompanied Florez on the trip until they reached the Garden Highway in Sutter County. She then told Florez to dump the box into the Sacramento River.

"Its just junk," Dorothea said.

Months later, a fisherman would discover the box sitting on the bank of the river. Police would open the box to reveal a horrendously decomposed body of an elderly man.

Everson Gillmouth.

But it would be three years before police would be able to positively identify Gillmouth. Dorothea would continue to cash his social security checks. She would write his family on his behalf, stating that he was "sick" and could not contact them himself.

NEW BOARDING HOME, SAME RULES

Puente would rent a different boarding home from the Odorico family in what would later be infamously called the "F Street Boarding House."

Dorothea charmed the Odorico family, keeping the house spotless. They thought of her as family and referred to her as "tia" (Spanish for aunt). Despite being unlicensed and on parole, Dorothea was allowed to manage the place and supervise tenants.

But Dorothea's reputation grew in the community. She gave to charities and went out of her way to help certain people when it attended to her needs. She went to a charity ball and California Governor Jerry Brown stepped across the room to kiss her on the cheek.

The Governor then asked her to dance to the delight of onlookers.

In 1986, Puente would strike a deal with social worker Peggy Nickerson in an effort to provide a home for senior citizens on fixed incomes.

"She was the best the system had to offer," Nickerson said as she referred over nineteen elderly people to Puente in two years.

Dorothea would be a "Godsend" to social workers because she had no qualms about accepting troubled tenants, elderly and disabled people who could be abusive and addicted to drugs.

But Dorothea simply wanted their money. By having them as her boarders, she would collect their money first and pay them as she saw fit. Parole agents would come and talk to Dorothea. They would order Dorothea to stay away from her senior citizen clientele to no avail. Dorothea was never cited.

"The parole agents definitely dropped the ball," Orange said. "They are overwhelmed with work but it was almost as if they turned a blind eye. Here was a woman who had a criminal record of forging checks, running a brothel, and stealing Social Security checks from the elderly. Somehow, someway, she was allowed to run a boarding house. It boggles the mind really but shows you how each part of the social system had a piece of the puzzle but no one connected the dots."

Puente played good cop and bad cop to her tenants. There were some who said she was cheap and detailed instances where she withheld both their mail and their money. But there were others who said she could be kind and would praise her cooking.

Despite her philanthropic veneer, Dorothea had an autocratic personality. If one of her tenants showed up late for a meal, they would be denied food. She would send them away then make the other tenants "say Grace" before the meal.

She also did not drive and used a local tax driver to shuttle her around town.

"She had a lot of rules," Dorothea's driver Patty Rohrbach said. "Number one, be punctual. Number two, do what I tell you. And we'll get a long just great. She was generous almost to a fault. She'd tip very nicely and make sure there was enough time on the meter to make it worth my while."

Dorothea had a routine. She would go to the local hardware store to get gardening supplies, then get groceries. On Sundays, she would go to church then go to bars to solicit possible clientele.

"Dorothea would target the down and out," Orange said. "She would go to bars and offer a listening ear to someone who looked disabled or elderly. She knew how to game the system and would give the person tips on how to collect more on their Social Security or disability check. Then she would hand them her business card and invite them to stay with her as a boarder."

"She called them 'throwaway people,'" Rohrbach recalled. "She said 'everyone has abandoned them and I've taken them in.' And I thought it was a charitable situation created for people who had nowhere else to go."

Rohrbach wasn't the only one taken in by Dorothea's facade. Social worker Nickerson brought a man named Bert Montoya to live in Dorothea's boarding home. She had taken special interest in Montoya as the 50-year-old Costa Rican needed a place to stay desperately. He was an alcoholic schizophrenic, a man who constantly "heard voices in his head" but someone who Nickerson perceived as a "sweet, kind man."

"Montoya had been living in a place called 'Detox,'" Orange said. "A shack of a homeless shelter that had little more than vinyl mattresses on concrete."

Dorothea took to Montoya almost immediately, sensing he was a lost soul in a teddy bear's body. Montoya had a kind spirit, he once found over two hundred dollars at a homeless shelter and turned it in. He was troubled but not dangerous.

He was someone Dorothea could take advantage of.

Dorothea would take Montoya around the home and introduce him to the other residents. First there was John McCauley, a loud mouth drunk that did all of Dorothea's bidding. Second was Ben Fink, another alcoholic who despite being Jewish had a swastika tattoo on his arm. Lastly, there was John Sharpe, a compulsive gambler who suffered from short term memory loss.

"Dorothea took Bert Montoya under her wing," Orange said. "Moreso than the other tenants. He liked the fact that he could call her 'momma' and she called him her 'honey bear.' The social worker was surprised at how well he had adjusted to living under Puente's care. But Dorothea used him as a trophy. She used him to show everyone how compassionate and nurturing she could be."

The other tenants began getting jealous of Bert, in particular, John McCauley.

"The other tenants were paying upwards of $300 a month," Orange said. "They would get room and board plus two hot meals. Bert would get all that for free. All because Dorothea had taking a liking to the kind yet simple-minded man."

Dorothea went so far as to set up Bert with a running tab at the local bar. Bert would come in to the tavern, drink no more than three beers, then be on his way.

As much as Dorothea took to Bert as her showpiece, Ben Fink was a thorn in her side.

Fink would drunk himself into a stupor and had an uncanny ability to achieve alcohol levels that would be enough to kill an elephant, let alone a human being.

One night, the compulsive John Sharp was watching a horror movie in his room when he heard a large thump. The sound came from the upstairs bedroom that belonged to Ben Fink. Then he heard large bumps coming down the steps, as if someone were dragging a body. He thought it creepy at the time but didn't investigate.

Ben Fink would then disappear from the boarding house.

No one thought anything of it, however, as boarding house occupants were a transient group of people. Dorothea herself would kick people out after a few weeks and sometimes tenants themselves would leave on their own accord.

Dorothea never liked Ben Fink. Bert Montoya was until one night he did something to get into her doghouse.

Bert had went to the local tavern and this time he had gotten so drunk that he passed out inside the bar. Three of the other tenants had to carry him back to the boarding house.

"The group of men that brought him back described Bert as 'blowing bubbles' through his mouth," Orange said. "So that opens up the possibility that he had something else in his system aside from alcohol. We could easily surmise that Dorothea had begun to drug him up and the alcohol only exacerbated his symptoms. But something had spooked Bert. Something prompted him to drink more than his usual amount. He was trying to medicate himself and forget something he had seen at the boarding house."

Bert then ran away from the home, walking miles in order to return to 'Detox', the homeless shelter downtown.

"I don't want to go back," Bert cried out when the Detox manager allowed him back into the home. "I don't want to go back."

WHAT IS THAT SMELL?

Tenants in the boarding house began complaining about a rancid smell that was coming from the empty bedroom upstairs.

This would later be labeled as the "Death Room".

When the owners of the home, the Odoricos, came to do their monthly inspection they couldn't help but notice the odor themselves.

"It smelled rotten," Ricardo said. "It smelled rotten in there."

"I thought it was the tenants,"said Laura Arebalo, Ricardo's daughter. "because some tenants they would not bath on a daily basis."

Dorothea deflected the complaints as expected. She would blame the neighbors, saying they must be cooking something that's "not right." Then when that sounded lame she would blame a broken sewage line.

But late at night, Dorothea would shampoo the carpet in the room, awaking John Sharp.

When tenants and the owner asked about the room, Dorothea would simply say it was a room that was "cursed."

It was the same room where her friend Ruth Monroe had died only a few years earlier.

Neighbors complained to the city and the Department of Health was called in. They did an inspection of the house and made Dorothea sign a few documents.

But the smell remained.

And Bert Montoya returned.

After over two weeks on the streets and sleeping at "Detox" he arrived back at Dorothea's door steps.

Bert wanted to slip back into the house unnoticed but Dorothea saw him.

"When they cross me," Dorothea said. "They don't cross me a second time."

Then Bert disappeared.

"There was a reason why Bert didn't want to go back to the house to begin with," Orange said. "He openly told the people at the Detox that he didn't want to go back. I think he saw something there. Mostly likely he saw them disposing of a body. Chopping up a corpse. Something had freaked him out and Dorothea knew he would eventually say something."

"Bert had become a problem for Dorothea," Sacramento Police Detective Cabrera said. "He might even bring the police. She couldn't allow Bert to bring attention to her. She apparently felt that there was only one thing to do."

MORE SUSPICIONS

Neighbors began taking note of the strange doings of a man only known as "Chief."

Dorothea thought of Chief as the resident handyman of the boarding home. She had the man do odd jobs around place even though he was an alcoholic. Neighbors saw that Chief carted off dirt and junk away in a wheelbarrow after digging in the basement of the boarding home. He then tore down a garage in the backyard and put in fresh cement.

Then Chief disappeared.

And the owners weren't pleased that Dorothea had put in a concrete patio without any consent on their part.

"One time I went to the house," Ricardo Odorico said. "And I found a concrete patio."

"I used to have lots of roses," Veronica Odorico said. "I liked roses. Then I went and saw that everything was different. I said (to Dorothea) 'What happened? You took out the roses. She said 'I don't like roses.' I used to tell my husband he gave her too much freedom. He said it was to improve the house. I said I liked it better like I had it before."

By May of 1988, neighbors no longer complained of a smell coming from Dorothea's home. Now they were complaining of a stench coming from Puente's backyard. Dorothea dismissed their concerns, telling them that she was using "fish emulsion" to fertilize her soil.

"We couldn't stand it," one neighbor said. "There was a sick smell in the air, and there were lots of flies in the area."

In November, of that same year, social worker Nickerson would arrive at Puente's boarding house to do a welfare check on her tenant, Bert Montoya.

Montoya had been last seen in August and Dorothea would tell the police that the man had "gone home to Mexico."

"Dorothea gave this huge elaborate story," Orange said. "But the social worker knew that Montoya would not have picked up and left without notifying her. Smelling something fishy, she notified the police."

Police initially believed Dorothea's story but returned after Nickerson stated that another one of her clients went missing after being in Puente's care.

"Dorothea was accommodating when the police came to question her," Orange said. "They could not do anything without her permission. They couldn't search the premises or even come inside her house. But she was very polite and allowed one of the detectives to look around the home. He found some medicine vials that looked suspicious. They had names of different tenants on the vials but they were all in one drawer of Dorothea's. Then the asked if they could look around in the garden. To his amazement, Dorothea remained cooperative and said it was okay."

The police began digging up Dorothea's back yard. Initially, the dig did not go well. The police unearthed eggshells, food and other articles of garbage. They discovered some leather-like material, with the detective describing it as "very opaque, leathery."

One of the detectives dug further and came upon what he thought was a tree root. He pulled on the "root" and broke it away.

It turned out to be a human leg bone.

And the leather-like material turned out to be decomposed flesh.

The police then discovered the first of several corpses on November 11th, 1988. They found two more the next day.

"It wasn't uncommon for old Victorian homes to have human remains in the backyard," Orange said. "People have dug holes in their backyards and have found bones that date back to the early 1900s. There were occasions where folks didn't have enough money for a proper burial so they buried bodies in the backyard to save money. Initially, that is what the police took the bones for. A case of an old time burial."

But news quickly spread throughout the town and people lined up around the home to gawk. The crowd swelled so large that the police had to cordon off the street. Hot dog and t-shirt vendors began to show up to sell their wares. One of the t-shirts had an elderly grandmother holding up a shovel. The caption on the shirt read "I dig Sacramento."

Dorothea then inquired with Detective Cabrera that she was going to "go for a cup of coffee" at the hotel. Cabrera himself walked her to the hotel to ensure that no one harassed her on the way.

The detective returned to the site and within twenty minutes, he unearthed another body.

"Where's Dorothea?" his Lieutenant asked.

"Dorothea would pay a cab driver sixty dollars to take her to Stockton," Orange said. "From there, she took a bus to Los Angeles."

The police remained on the premises and continued to dig. Three days later, they would unearth seven bodies. They would identify Ben Fink by his swastika tattoo. Dorothy Miller, an elderly alcoholic would be identified as well as Betty Palmer.

"One of the more gruesome finds was that of Betty Palmer," Orange said. "She had her hands and feet chopped off as well as her head. Police searched far and wide for her different body parts to no avail. They dug and even checked under the crawlspace of the house. It is believed that Palmer was Dorothea's second victim and she was perfecting her technique, removing whatever evidence of identification she could."

THE AFTERMATH

The police continued to search the boarding house but found no other bodies. They still believed that other murders took place and Puente had used other means to dispose of her victims.

"We are getting a large number of calls from people with relatives who have stayed there," the Sacramento Police said in an official statement. "There are a lot more than seven names."

Twenty five tenants of Puente were missing and unaccounted for as the police did forensic work on the seven corpses.

Meanwhile, Dorothea Puente remained on the run.

The search began for Puente and by November 17th, she had been spotted in a Los Angeles bar. She had introduced herself to a patron as "Donna Johansson" and began questioning the man about his disability income. She offered to move in with him and fix him "Thanksgiving dinner" despite only meeting the man.

"She invited the man back to her hotel," Orange said. "He found her charming but declined. She got up and left and he's watching television in the bar. A news report comes on and he sees Dorothea is wanted for murder."

The bar patron called the LAPD and Dorothea was arrested at her hotel. Detective Cabrera and other officials from Sacramento Police arrived in Los Angeles to take her back.

"I'm sorry, Detective," Dorothea said while sipping on a cup of coffee.

"Dorothea, I knew if we dig we're going to find more," Cabrera said. "I know that. I know that."

"Well, I didn't put them there," Dorothea said. "I couldn't drag a body any place."

"I believe that. But I believe there's somebody else involved here."

Cabrera knew that there was a distinct possibility that Dorothea had an accomplice.

"Bert Montoya weighed about two-hundred and fifty pounds," Cabrera said. "How does a person that's five-foot-three, five-foot-four, one hundred and thirty-five pounds carry somebody like that."

Resident John McCauley was arrested and questioned by the police. He was later released for lack of evidence.

The police went on to believe that Dorothea had unknowing accomplices, employing her tenants to dig the holes. She would cut the body into pieces. For the pieces she needed help with, she would roll the body part up in carpet or plastic and have someone carry it out.

THE DEATH ROOM

In December of 1988, forensic police work had positively identified four more victims that were uncovered at the Puente boarding home. The victims were Bert Montoya, Vera Martin, Dorothy Miller and Leona Carpenter.

There was evidence to believe that Carpenter was buried alive.

"She (Leona) was put in the ground shallow," Cabrera said. "It appears that her legs, the victim kicked her legs up. And in doing so compacted the dirt around her legs forming a little bridge."

The mystery remained about the smell of the "Death Room". There were no remains found in the room.

Yet the smell never went away.

"One thing I'll never forget is when I pulled the carpet back," Cabrera continued. "When I pulled it back, the most grotesque odor came out and I knew that it was putrefying body fluids. The thing is there was other people living there. And it (burying the bodies) was based on opportunity. When was the best opportunity to put the people in the ground. So these bodies would have to lie there (in the room) until a period or a time when she could get them into the ground. I was in those graves. There was no odor. There as no smell. But in the 'Death Room', the carpet. The body fluid had a smell that would knock you over....This was nothing more than a house of horrors."

THE MOTIVATION

The sum total of Puente's scheming and killing netted her more than $5,000 per month. In turn, she would take the clothing of her victims and donate them to charities.

"We would get calls from local charities," Cabrera recalled. "And they said they were given bags of clothing from Dorothea. Well, what a great way to get rid of evidence."

Dorothea would be brought to trial and prosecutors would describe her as one of the most "cold, calculating" serial killers in American history. No one ever witnessed her kill anybody but Dorothea would later reveal that she would use drugs to overdose her victims. Forensics would discover traces of a prescription strength sleeping pill in all of the remains.

The social security checks would continue to arrive at the residence despite the tenant being deceased.

Dorothea used part of her ill-gotten gains to get a facelift.

On December of 1993, Dorothea would be convicted on three counts of murder of the nine bodies discovered.

"The tragedy in looking back at this story is that it could have been prevented," Orange said. "No one took the time to investigate Dorothea's background. Different agencies knew different information about her yet no one collaborated. The true victims are, of course, the deceased. They were referred to Dorothea as the 'throwaway people'. People that when she dumped into the ground, no one came looking. The tragedy is that Dorothea was right. But for the circumstances surrounding the disappearance of Bert Montoya, who knows how many more murders she would have committed?"

She was sentenced to life in Chowchilla State Prison and she died in 2011.

DEATH ROW GRANNY

Georgia Johnson

It never ends.

No way.

No way am I letting this man demean and degrade me another day.

He's just like my father.

A binge drinker. And the binges were happening more and more.

He's on the road to nowhere and taking me with him.

It never ends.

First my father. Now him.

Fuck it.

I threw the cigarette on the blanket. I knew it was flammable.

Then I watched the smoke rise and smiled.

In Lumberton, North Carolina, Thomas Burke fell victim to a house fire which was caused by a burning cigarette. Investigative authorities thought that he had fallen asleep while smoking, leaving thirty-eight-year-old Velma Burke as his widow.

They didn't know that the fire was set by Velma.

Velma knew how to play the part of the grieving widow. She cried and gave the authorities the requisite crocodile tears. No one would believe that the murder of Thomas Burke would set off a series of killings performed by the seemingly kind and harmless church-going woman with the soft voice.

But Velma was a killer...

EARLY LIFE

Velma Bullard grew up as the second of nine children in the rural part of Sampson County, North Carolina.

Times were tough for the Bullard family. They would live on a small farm with no electricity, running water or an outhouse.

"They had to go outdoors," forensic psychologist Paula Orange said. "The entire family had to endure the indignity of going into the woods or using pots to shit and piss."

The home was small and cramped for the nine children. Velma would be forced to sleep in the same bedroom with her parents until the age of five.

Her father was a loom repairman (fixing an apparatus that was used to weave clothing) and an abusive alcoholic. Velma had an older brother, Olive, who were subject to his nightly beatings. Lillie, her mother, was too meek to protect her children from her husband's violent outbursts.

"She had the type of father who would not need any provocation," Orange said. "He would take out the pettiest frustrations, like not being able to find something around the house, and take it out on the children. Velma would become resentful toward her mother who was too weak or indifferent to stop her father from beating on the kids. She accepted his discipline as 'the way it was.'"

Velma would find school as a welcome escape from her dreadful home life. She loved her teacher and was an excellent student during her early grade school years. When she would return home from school, she took solace in the fact that her father would always arrive home late as he worked long hours at the textile mill.

"Her father Murphy had that Protestant work ethic in him," Orange said. "He accepted the long hours and low pay, seeing a kind of nobility in that. Only problem was, he would binge drink. Not store bought alcohol but homemade moonshine. After a couple of shots, he would be 'lit' and inflict his wrath on everyone in the house."

By the age of eleven, Velma would be forced to take on various chores around the farm. She would clean up the house, washing and iron everyone's clothing (eleven people). Her father would chastise her for not mending or sewing his work clothes properly as well.

"Her father was a stern taskmaster," Orange said. "Hell, you can say 'slave driver.' He would have Velma come home early from school days when the laundry got too backed up. Velma hated this and felt embarrassed. Her family didn't have much and as she grew older her classmates began to see her for what she was, a poor girl that was an easy mark for teasing."

Velma would grow to be 5'3" but gain weight as she got older. She would be mocked about her obesity, her shoddy clothes the gap between her two front teeth. She would also be called "knot head" after she ran head first into a boy at school which left a permanent contusion on her forehead.

By the age of twelve, Velma seemed to have taken on all of her mother's duties. She would cook all of the family meals in addition to performing cleaning around the farm house. She would miss school for days at a time as her father forced her to complete chores around the home before she could continue her education.

"Academic achievement was not at the forefront of her father's mind," Orange said. "Her mother was of little use because of her depression and mental illness. Velma was the oldest girl so she took on the duties of mom at an age where she should have been playing with dolls."

ANGER, ABUSE, AND CHURCH

Despite her father's verbal abuse and alcohol-fueled beatings, the family kept up a face of religious interest. Velma would be sent to Bible school every year until the age of thirteen. During her last year of Bible school, her father marked the occasion by buying Velma a silk pink dress with ribbons. Velma recalled the day as one of the happiest of her life.

The happiness would be short-lived.

Velma would claim that her father raped her when she was thirteen years old. She revealed this only to her pastor in her later years before she stood trial. Velma did not even tell her mother whom she did not think would believe the molestation took place.

"Things that went on inside our home when I grew up," Velma said. "Were kept inside."

At the age of fifteen, Velma continued to excel in school. Despite her chubby physique, she becomes adept at basketball and is pegged to be the team's star player for the upcoming season. But her father did not allow her to play.

"Who is going to iron these damn clothes?" he snarled.

The family then moved to Robeson county and switched from the Presbyterian denomination to Baptist. It was here that Velma would meet Thomas Burke and the two made it clear that they wanted to date. Once again, Velma's father would intervene, telling Velma that she had to wait until her sixteenth birthday until she could date.

The two waited patiently for her birthday to arrive and the following year Thomas would propose to her while they went to the movies.

Knowing that her father would not approve, Velma and Thomas eloped, moving to Dillon, South Carolina. Neither Thomas or Velma had any money as they both quit high school to get married. Thomas then went to work at a local textile mill.

"At this point, I believe that Velma began to realize that her life would not be that much better with Thomas," Orange said. "He literally has the same job as her father."

Economics forced Velma and Thomas to move in with his parents. This arrangement would last for a year until Thomas got a better paying job at a soft drink company.

At the age of nineteen, Velma would give birth to her first son, Ronnie. The couple would then move back to Parkton, North Carolina where they would remain in the same home for eleven years. Two years later, the young couple would welcome a daughter named Kim.

A CYCLE OF RELIGION AND ABUSE

The Burkes would be fixtures at the local Baptist church with Velma taking the reigns to teach a Sunday school class. But the prayers and sermons would do little to offset the growing ennui in the Burke home. Two years after giving birth to Kim, Velma would get hit by a drunk driver while crossing the street. She would be hospitalized for an extended period, suffering both physically and mentally.

Thomas' job at the soft drink company would not be enough to provide for the family. Velma would be forced to leave her small children at home and work in a textile mill just like her father. The couple would have different work hours, with Velma working nights and Thomas working days as they would take turns watching the children.

Velma would fall victim to the hard work at the mill and the stress of raising two young children. She began bleeding and her doctor performed a hysterectomy.

Velma's mother would take pity on the couple and give them one acre of land near their old farm. Thomas would build a three-bedroom home for the family but Velma was already going down a slippery slope. Her personality changed after the hysterectomy, claiming that she always felt "nervous and afraid."

Things would get worse as Thomas suffered a head injury in a car accident. He then began to drink heavily and begin to beat Velma.

"It was deja vu," Orange said. "Velma had, in essence, married her father."

One night, the couple argued and Thomas punched Velma in an alcohol-fueled tantrum. The police are called to the home and Velma sent Thomas to the state hospital to get treatment for his drinking. Her husband remains there for three days but when he returns home, his behavior is worse than behavior. He's angry at Velma for sending him to the "drunk tank". His alcoholism worsens and he would go on to lose his job because of absenteeism.

"Velma is thirty-five years old at this time," Orange said. "But she's an old thirty-five with crow's feet under her eyes and a hangdog look. She's had a rough life, not necessarily by her own design, and it has taken its toll."

Velma leaves the textile mill but then finds two different jobs in order to support the family. During the day, she works as a sales clerk in a Belk department store. At night, she goes to work as a machine operator in a cotton mill.

Thomas, meanwhile, would continue to drink.

He rages on a daily basis, on one occasion he pinned son Ronnie up against the wall and threatened him with a knife. Velma would faint during the encounter and be transported to the hospital. She was diagnosed as having a nervous breakdown and lapsed into a serious depression. The medical staff gave her tranquilizers to calm down. Velma believed that it was during this stint in the hospital that she became addicted to the painkillers.

"The drugs were helping," Orange said. "When nothing else did. So she wanted more and more."

Velma's children acknowledged that their mother's mood swings were due to the drugs.

Over the next three years, Velma would go in and out of the hospital for drug overdoses. After each visit, her addiction only grew as did her prescription list.

"She fell through the cracks in her own family," Orange said. "And in the system itself. Her family had their own issues to deal with as Thomas would abuse everyone on a daily basis. Finally, Velma did something she could control. She killed her husband."

On April 21st, 1969, Velma would drop a cigarette on the floor of her home and waited until her husband inhaled enough smoke to die.

His death, however, would do nothing to solve Velma's problems.

Her addictions and anxiety would only get worse.

A HOSPITAL FREQUENT FLYER

Velma would have another nervous breakdown after killing Thomas and lapse into a guilt-ridden depression. But seven months later, a co-worker at the Belk department store would introduce her to fifty-four-year-old Jennings Barfield. Jennings had emphysema and diabetes but Velma would marry him anyway. Unlike her marriage with Thomas which started out well, Velma's marriage with the older Jennings would be troubled from the start. Her drug addiction would escalate and Jennings would express his own regret at marrying her.

"I don't know why I married her," Jennings said. "All she does is pop pills all day."

After less than three years of marriage, Velma decided to part ways with Jennings. She didn't file for divorce, however, she decided to poison him with arsenic. She would later claim that she only meant to "make him sick."

Jennings Barfield was already ill and doctors had no suspicion that Velma was behind the death. Arsenic was a slow burn poison that could kill without detection. The autopsy called for no arsenic test and Velma had gotten away with murder once again.

But Seven months later, Velma would overdose on her prescription meds and become hospitalized. Her family recognized the pattern but could not wean Velma off of the drinks. She would remain hospitalized for three weeks.

Her personality seemed to change after the hospital release. She returned to work at Belk department store but kept being combative and argumentative with customers. Her boss knew of her circumstances and tried to coax her to do better. He took her away from the public contact and into the back stock room where he had her put pricing on the clothing items.

Her boss soon realized that Velma's addiction had gotten out of control. Velma would not be able to function in the back room, leaving tasks uncompleted as she would have her prescription medications delivered to the store.

"It is a hopeless situation," the store manager told Velma's son Ronnie before he fired his mother.

BROKE AND DESTITUTE

With no income, Velma would lose the family home as she no longer paid the mortgage. She would be forced to move back in with her parents and face the two people she blamed everything for.

Her father had grown ill, however, and would die from lung cancer shortly after Velma moved back into the home. She would feel bad about her father's death and admit that she had a love/hate relationship with him.

"I had learned to love him as much as I had hated him," Velma said. "He was so good to my kids. I think he tried to do with my kids like he wished he had done to us. He could not stand to see me correct them. If I would pick them up and spank them, he would ask me, 'Isn't that enough?'"

But after her father's death Velma self-medicated once again. She overdosed and was hospitalized for two weeks. Her family didn't judge, they instead thought she was "cursed."

"Velma needed psychiatric help," Orange said. "So she began medicating herself with deleterious results. She would "doctor shop" for different physicians who would be manipulated into giving her the drugs she wanted. Her addiction eventually grows until she becomes desperate for money in order to fuel the drug habit."

A MURDERER AND A THIEF

Velma began stealing from those closest to her, starting with her mother. Her mother confronted Velma about a missing check and Velma went ballistic.

"She had violent mood swings," Orange said. "The medication had completely changed her personality as she needed the drugs above all else. The people around her were not familiar with how to handle a person who had this kind of mental illness. So this made for a very dangerous cocktail for her and anyone close to her."

Hitting a new low, Velma took out a $1,000 loan under her mother Lillie's name. She put up the family home as collateral and forged her mother's signature on the documents. Velma then blew through the money and a month later took out another loan, once again using her mother's house as collateral. The following month, she emptied the checking account on her now deceased husband, Jennings. Two months later, the loan company began sending Velma overdue notices as she had not been paying off the loan.

"In Velma's mind," Orange said. "She had no other choice but to kill off her own mother."

Velma went to the local pharmacy and looked for bottles that had the warning of "fatal if ingested." She put the poison into a drink for her mother and watched as she drank the fatal elixir.

Her mother then began vomiting and lost control of her bowels. Within a few hours, her mother could not so much as walk and an ambulance was called.

Velma came to visit her in the hospital to finish the job. Armed with a Thermos, she made a special concoction of chicken soup and arsenic.

"Drink it slow," Velma said as she tenderly lifted the cups to the lips of her ailing mother. "Slow."

Her mother would eventually die of "natural causes" as no one suspected Velma of committing murder. Instead, she received sympathy.

"So sorry for your loss," hospital staff said.

"The thing with arsenic is that it shuts down the whole system," Orange said. "So hospital staff just chalked up her mother's weakness to old age. Checking for arsenic poisoning would be the furthest thing from their mind."

Velma showed the necessary emotion and received sympathy from friends and family. She then moved in with her daughter Kim and son-in-law Dennis who lived in a trailer park. She could not evade the authorities for long though as the authorities caught wind of Velma's check forgeries.

Velma reacted as she always did. She would run away and medicate herself.

"Her drug addiction kept pushing her into a corner and she saw no way out," Orange said. "So, this time, she goes to her son Ronnie's house and overdoses again, trying to kill herself. She falls and breaks her collar bone which laid her out in the hospital another three weeks."

But the police find her situation unsympathetic.

"We're sorry, Velma," the deputy informed her at her hospital bed. "But once you have been cleared for release, we will arrest you."

Velma would not have that. She tried to overdose again but this go around the hospital staff pumped out her stomach.

She was sent to court the next day and sentenced to six months in jail for the forgery. She is released after four months for good behavior.

NO REHAB HERE

Her addiction still unchecked, Velma returned to live with Kim and her son-in-law. She rummaged through the belongings of her son-in-law and stole a check, forging his name so she can get more prescription meds. Her daughter Kim now has caught wind of her mother's addiction, pleading with her doctors to stop prescribing her.

"In some ways," Orange said. "The doctors were just as guilty as she was. But back in the day, there was no way to cross-reference this stuff like we do now. Once she had her fill with one doctor she would go to the next and the next."

Velma's addiction prevented her from taking a forty-hour a week job. So she looked for alternative forms of income.

She would find a job taking care of the elderly.

Montgomery and Dolly Edwards would be her first clients.

"She found herself some easy targets," Orange said. "There didn't seem to be any legislative body in place that prevents sociopaths from caretaking the elderly. So Velma doesn't slip through any cracks, she just befriends the elderly couple and begins taking care of them."

Montgomery was blind and unable to walk. He was 93-years old and his 83-year old wife was too feeble to take care of him. They paid $75 a week for Velma to become their live-in caretaker.

All was good, at least in the beginning. But Dolly had a sharp tongue and would criticize Velma daily. Velma would keep a nice exterior unless confronted, saw Dolly has yet another wheel in her cycle of verbal abuse.

"It seemed to be a never-ending loop for her," Orange said. "Being forced to deal with verbally abusive people. Velma had long since snapped and Dollie simply had no idea who she was dealing with."

Velma began to plot out Montgomery and Dollie's demise until she meets their nephew, Stuart Taylor.

Stuart was already married but was blown away when he met the caretaker of his Aunt Dollie.

Velma would play it cool, stealing what she could from the couple in terms of petty cash and household items that had value. They outlived their usefulness to her within a year as Montgomery died of "natural causes". One month later, Dolly also passed away.

And again, no one suspected the sweet and soft-spoken Velma to have had anything to do with their deaths.

MOVING ON

Velma saw being a caretaker as a perfect front for her. She could steal as much money as she could and when the old folks detected something amiss she would simply poison them. After killing the Edwards' couple, she set the word out at church that she as available to be a caregiver. The pastor would refer her to Margie Lee Pittman who was seeking for a caregiver for her elderly parents, John Henry and Record Lee.

"She comes here twice a week," the pastor reassured Pittman. "She's a nice, kindly woman. You can't go wrong."

Pittman's father, John Henry Lee, was eighty years old when he discovered that his new caregiver had forged a $50 check on his account. He then fell violently ill, suffering through a spastic spell of vomiting, diarrhea, and convulsions. The doctors would chalk up his quick death to gastroenteritis but in fact, he had been poisoned with arsenic.

Velma played the caregiver role until his end. She attended his funeral and cried with the family, sending an ornate wreath (with money stolen from the dead man) to the proceedings.

For whatever reason, Velma spared Lee's wife and moved back to Lumberton, North Carolina to live in a trailer park. She began working as an aide in a nursing home and received word from Stuart that he was now a widow. The two began dating and she moved part of her belongings into his home.

"Stuart is a nice guy," Orange said. "He has no idea what kind of woman Velma is. She is so manipulative and cunning that the younger man is putty in her hands. So the relationship starts great as she reels him in with kindness and charm."

The couple are happy cohabitating until Stuart Stuart finds a letter addressed to Velma from the state penitentiary.

Curious, he began reading the correspondence and realized that is from a former cellmate of Velma.

Stuart became enraged. He threatened to "expose" Velma to all of his family and friends. Somehow, someway, however, she was able to calm him down.

He then found out that she had forged over $200 in checks on his account. The two argued but stayed together for the next two months.

"Velma had the Christian facade down pat," Orange said. "She asked Stuart to forgive her and the next thing you know they are going to a Rex Humbard revival. But before they went, she poured arsenic poison in both his beer and tea. She made sure he drank every drop."

Returning home from the revival, Stuart started to vomit on the drive home, the poison kicking in.

Velma had to keep the con going. She had to appear like a concerned girlfriend so she called up Stuart's daughter, Alice, later that night and told her that Stuart had came down with the flu.

Stuart's daughter expressed concern but Velma kept her at bay.

"Don't you worry now, honey. I'll take care of everything."

Stuart died the next day.

Velma would speak at Stuart's funeral and tearfully asked for his wedding band. His family graciously allowed her to have it and gave her $400 to help her cope with the grief.

But Alice knew her father was a picture of health. She vociferously argued for more tests beyond the standard autopsy and sure enough, arsenic had been found in Stuart's tissues.

On March 10th, 1978, the sheriffs arrived at Velma's home to bring her in for questioning. She was interrogated for over three hours, holding her ground. But she knows the evidence will trump her denials and tries to commit suicide after being released. This go around, however, her son Ronnie stopped her.

The sheriffs come to visit Velma again and she has one more surprise up her sleeve.

But Velma has one more surprise up her sleeve.

She would confess. Not only for the murder of Stuart but of six others.

"I set my first husband on fire," Velma confessed without an attorney present. "And I killed the rest of them."

"It was almost as if she wanted to be free of the guilt she had been carrying," Orange said. "Her confession seemed to take a burden off her back."

"The last ten years were like that," Velma said. "A drug nightmare. It was a case of not knowing where you are or what you've done."

The bodies of her victims were later exhumed and all tested positive for arsenic.

FACING THE GRIM REAPER

Velma's case would be prosecuted by Joe Freeman Britt, who was listed in the Guinness Book of World Records as the country's "deadliest prosecutor."

Velma would plead not guilty by reason of insanity but the court denied her plea.

"I needed to keep them sick until I could pay back the money I had stolen from them," Velma said. "I wanted to earn their thanks by nursing them back to health. I needed the money. I was addicted to pain killers. Anti-depressants. Amphetamines."

On November 23rd, 1978, Velma's trial would begin in Elizabethtown, North Carolina where she would be charged with the first-degree murder of her boyfriend, Stuart Taylor. The trial lasted seven days and the jury reached a verdict of guilty, placing her on death row at the age of 47. She was scheduled to be executed on February 3rd, 1979 but received a stay.

Velma would be sentenced to death and the verdict was appealed all the way to the U.S. Supreme court. Her attorney maintained that the jury had never been presented with the full extent of Velma's "addiction and background." Velma remained tight-lipped about that to everyone but her pastor. Her attorney felt thought her horrific background could have been used as part of her defense and the jury would have found her to be more of a sympathetic case.

CHANGING SPOTS?

"She's not the same person who went to prison in 1978," Kim Burke Norton, Velma's daughter said.

While in jail, Velma became a model prisoner.

"The first week I was here was the worst week," Velma recalled. "Everything about it."

Velma no longer had access to her drugs in prison and she began to dry out. With daily visits from two different pastors, Velma began to discuss her anger and repressed issues that fueled her addiction and murders.

Velma would claim that as she was awaiting trial in 1978 she came to a "meeting with Christ" that caused her to "change inwardly."

Velma heard a broadcast by radio evangelist JK Kinkle. "Jesus loves you, prisoners, too," Kinkle said. "He died for you too. No matter what you've done, the Lord will forgive you."

After Velma heard this sermon, she dropped to her knees and cried out to God.

She would then become the "go to" counselor for young inmates in the prison.

The inmates would nickname Velma as "Mama Margie" because of her wisdom and she would in turn think of them as her "adopted children."

The prison guards and counselors would take the most incorrigible prisoners and place them in a cell next to Velma. Velma would invariably counsel the young prisoner and advise them on the correct path.

"They'd come in ready to kill themselves," Sister Mary Teresa Floyd said. "And here she was with a death sentence, mothering and helping them."

"Living in prison is a struggle," Velma said. "Even at its best. And I know that without Him and His strength that has sustained me, I couldn't have made it even this far."

Her stay on death row soon became a part of the news brief. During this time, a phalanx of evangelists would take her cause to the mainstream. The Reverend Hugh Hoyle would become Velma's personal minister as she received stays of execution in September, October and December of 1981. She would also have a letter correspondence with Ruth Graham, Billy Graham's wife as well as meeting their daughter Ann.

While Velma impressed the Christian do-gooders, the family members of the victims were not taken in by her "conversion."

"She's got religion now, they say," Margie Lee Pittman said. "Well, she had religion before. So we all thought."

A few more stays were granted until 1984 when the U.S. Supreme Court justice Warren Burger granted her a stay until August of that year. At this point, however, her execution seemed inevitable. In an ironic move, Velma would choose poison rather than the gas chamber and enjoyed the final visits from her children and grandchildren.

During the final week before her execution, the Reverend Hoyle, and his wife came to the prison with a battery-powered portable keyboard. His wife played the little organ then the Reverend sang "He Hideth My Soul" and "He is So precious to Me" in the cramped visitor booth.

Velma sang along, whistling in the graveyard before the reaper came for her.

She then wrote letters to each of the victim's family asking them for forgiveness. Reverend Hoyle would deliver the letters to the families, all of whom would refuse them.

MEET THE HANGMAN

As her execution date neared, Velma was placed in a solitary cell that stood directly across from the death chamber.

"It's total isolation," Velma said. "From everyone I had been with for six years."

North Carolina Governor James B. Hunt would reject her final plea for clemency.

On the day of her execution, the jail house would turn into a media frenzy. Death penalty advocates gathered outside the prison and chanted "Hip, hip, hurrah...K-I-L-L" while some sloganeered with "burn, bitch, burn". The protesters held up a few placards that quote Romans ch.13 which ironically was a verse that Velma would repeat to guards during her prison stay.

"For rulers are not a terror to good works, but to the evil…(The ruler) beareth no the sword in vain, for he is the minister of God, a revenger to execute wrath upon him that doeth evil."

The execution was scheduled to take place at 2:00 a.m but the protesters remained outside, their chants reduced to a simple "Kill her! Kill her!"

On November 2nd, 1984, Velma would be executed by lethal injection. The prison official came out and addressed the press, giving out copies of Barfield's statement of apology. The reporters then eagerly anticipated what Velma requested for her last meal. Initially, Velma just wanted the normally scheduled prison food; chicken livers, collard greens and a sheet cake with peanut butter icing. The last meal was delivered but Velma immediately lost her appetite. Instead, she opted for Cheese Doodles and a glass of Coca-Cola.

"Her attorney believed that Velma could have done some good in life," Orange said. "He stated that she could have become a teacher, counselor or a pastor. But her father set her on a path of self-destruction that she couldn't escape from. By the time she the left that road to ruin, she was too far gone in terms of her murderous acts. Justice had to be served in the end. In the end, the law doesn't care how genuine you are in your pleas for forgiveness. It only cares about the rule of law."

"I'm sorry for the hurt that I've caused," Velma said before her execution. "So many people, today if it were possible, I wish I could take every bit of hurt on myself."

THE MURDER OF BROOKE WILBERGER

82

OLIVIA WATSON

Chapter 1

May 24, 2004 is a day many people in Corvallis, Oregon will never forget. It was the day a drunk man who was also high on crack set forth to destroy a life. Joel Courtney set out that morning in his 1997 green Dodge Caravan in search of a young, pretty co-ed to fulfill his dark fantasies. He cruised through the Oregon State University campus, searching, failing. But Courtney was persistent, and his wishes were soon fulfilled after he came across the Oak Park apartment complex a block down the road.

On the same morning, Brooke Wilberger woke up without any inclination that this might be her final day on Earth. She was newly home after finishing her first year of University, and was enjoying how sunny the spring had turned out to be. She headed over to the Oak Park apartment complex, which her sister managed, to help do some cleaning and basic repairs. Her sister needed help washing the lightposts out in the parking lot, so Wilberger grabbed some rags and a bucket of soapy water and got to work.

A few minutes into her work, Wilberger noticed a green van pull up. Inside, a man was waving an envelope at her, trying to get her attention. He looked like he needed help, so Wilberger approached. When the van pulled away seconds later, all that was left of Brooke was the soapy water and her now-broken flip flops.

It would be more than five years before Brooke Wilberger came home, but she would never come home alive. The story of her disappearance was a twisted tale full of hope, but it would only ever have a bittersweet ending.

Chapter 2

Brooke Wilberger was born in Fresno, California on February 20, 1985. She was the youngest of six. With three older sisters and two older brothers, she lived in a busy household, but it was a pleasant place to live. Her parents, Greg and Cammy Wilberger, were devout

Mormons, and raised their children to be the same. The family was incredibly close-knit.

Brooke Wilberger grew to be quite a beautiful, accomplished young woman. Besides boasting a strong set of mormon morals, she also excelled in school and had a lot of friends. The tall, thin blonde also received a lot of attention from the guys in her school, but she seldom dated.

The summer before Brooke began high school, the Wilberger family left California behind and moved North to Eugene, Oregon. Here, Brooke attended Elmira High School, and met her first serious boyfriend, Justin Blake. Blake also came from a mormon family, and was devoted to his religion, so the couple got along famously. They respected each other's minds, bodies, and faith.

The young couple graduated together in 2003, and while they were both dedicated to each other, they were on different paths towards the future. Wilberger wanted to go right to college so she could better equip herself with the knowledge she would need to turn around and better those in need around her. Blake was ready to jump into missionary work.

Wilberger was accepted into the Brigham Young University in Provo, Utah, and when she set off for her freshman year there, Blake set off for Venezuela to participate in a Mormon missionary campaign.

Although she was separated from her first love, Wilberger could not deny how happy she was at Brigham Young. The University was owned and operated by the Church of Jesus Christ of Latter Day Saints, and was the largest religious university in the country. She was immersed in her faith in new experiences and knowledge. She was actively participating in something much larger than herself, and she loved it.

Wilberger kept in constant contact with her family while away at University. She would often call and tell them about what she was learning, who she was meeting, and what she was doing. Her favorite topic of conversation, though, was always the inspiration her surroundings gave her to do better for the world. Although she was excited to see her family after the end of the year, she was in no rush to leave the busy, bustling campus for small-town Oregon.

After finishing her classes for the year, Brooke returned home to her family in late April of 2004. Her parents still lived in Eugene, but she wanted to maintain some of her freedom, so Brooke often stayed with her sister, Stephanie, who lived an hour outside of Eugene in an apartment complex she managed in Corvallis.

Her family were ecstatic to have her back home, close by, where they believed she would be safe.

Chapter 3

On May 24, 2004, Brooke had been home for about a month. She was staying with her sister in the Oak Park apartments, which were just down the road from Oregon State University, where summer classes were already in full swing.

That morning, a female student of Oregon State named Randy was walking through the Reser Stadium parking lot when she noticed a green van driving around her. When it pulled up next to her, the driver of the van got out and asked Randy for directions. The student had a bad feeling about the man, and when she looked in the back seat of the van she noticed a bunch of empty boxes and blankets. Before the man could get too close, Randy excused herself and hurried off to class.

Several minutes later, another student, Crystal, was approached by the same van in the same parking lot. Crystal did speak to the man, who again asked for directions, but the conversation was interrupted by an athletic's coach, who Randy had reported the earlier incident to. When confronted by the coach, the van's driver quickly jumped back into his vehicle and sped off of the campus.

While this was all happening, Brooke Wilberger was a block down the road from Reser Stadium at the Oak Park apartment complex. That morning she was planning on helping her sister Stephanie do some routine maintenance work on the complex. She decided to start with washing the lamp posts in the parking lot, so she grabbed a bucket, filled it with soapy water, and headed outside. Stephanie saw Brooke hard at work scrubbing the lamp posts at 10:00 a.m. It was the last time she ever saw her sister alive.

Shortly after 10:00 a.m., the same green van that had been causing havoc on the Oregon State campus pulled into the Oak Park apartment complex. The van pulled up to Brooke, blocking her view of the apartments. He began asking for directions, but when Brooke drew near, he pulled out a knife and forced the 19-year-old into the back seat of his van and sped away.

Five minutes down the road, the van pulled over and it's driver, Joel Courtney, got out and bound Wilberger's arms and legs with duct tape. He also covered her body with blankets he had stashed in the back seat. After this, he sped off towards a nearby area that was covered with heavy forestation.

Hours after Brooke was snatched from the apartment complex, her sister Stephanie realized that she hadn't seen or heard from her in a while. She decided to track her down to make sure she was okay, and began with the place she had last seen her—the complex's parking lot. When she got there she was surprised to see an almost empty parking lot, save for the cleaning supplies Brooke had been using and Brookes flip flop sandals, one of which was now broken.

Stephanie immediately ran inside and called police, who immediately launched a missing person's case despite their protocol stating they should wait 24-hours first. Brooke's broken flip flops at her last known location triggered enough of an alarm.

When detectives arrived at the Oak Park apartments, they quickly discovered that her truck, purse, phone, and wallet were all still at the apartments. If she had left the apartments by herself, she had done so without any identification, money, and shoes. It seemed unlikely that this would have been the case.

The search for Brooke began in the same way most crimes do—with the victim's significant other. In this case, Brooke's long-term boyfriend was quickly eliminated because he was over 4000 miles away doing missionary work in Venezuela. Brooke's family was also quickly ruled out.

During this process, the word of Brooke's disappearance quickly got out to the community, and a massive volunteer search was launched by the Wilberger's Mormon church. Within days of Brooke's disappearance, both Eugene and Corvallis were covered in missing posters detailing Brooke's physical appearance and last known location. Over 4000 acres of heavily-wooded area outside of Corvallis was searched for any signs of the missing girl over eleven days. None were found.

Police soon began to realize that the best chance they had of finding Wilberger would be to find the person who had taken her from the Oak Park apartments, so they quickly began to focus on the few early leads they had in the case.

The method in which Wilberger was abducted led police to believe that her abductor was a repeat offender. It's difficult to grab a grown woman off of the streets without anyone seeing or hearing anything. Police began looking through sex offender registries and crime logs to create a suspect pool, one that turned out to include over one thousand names, all of whom were interviewed.

One of the first people contacted by police was 45-year-old ex-con Lauren Hugo Krueger. He had been convicted in 1985 for attempted rape and had served time for the felony assault and kidnapping of a 23-year-old jogger. Krueger had also been questioned in relation to several reports of harassment and stalking. Most damningly, Krueger had also been spotted at a car dealership less than a block away from where Wilberger was abducted from. It was a promising start to the investigation.

Chapter 4

Many police officers in Corvallis believed they may have identified the man who abducted Brooke Wilberger on May 24, 2004, as being Lauren Krueger. He had committed several similar crimes in the past, making him a likely suspect. However, when he was interviewed, police discovered he had an airtight alibi for that afternoon, and he was eliminated in the case.

Shortly after Krueger was eliminated as a suspect, another man by the name of Sun Koo King was identified as a probably suspect. King was an Oregon State graduate who was unemployed and lived in the area. He had recently had a lot of trouble with the law for breaking and entering into Oregon State dorm rooms and stealing their occupants underwear.

Detectives searched King's home and found a startling collection of women's underwear, used tampons, and pubic hair. King also catalogued where he found each object of his collection, which allowed investigators to see that he had gotten most of the items from dorms at the University and from the laundry room at the Oak Park apartments, the same apartments Brooke Wilberger lived in with her sister.

Police were shocked by what they found at King's home, but what shocked them more was that there seemed to be no sign of Brooke Wilberger anywhere. Further, King passed a polygraph test and seemed to have an airtight alibi. Investigators were again forced to abandon the promising lead.

By October 2004, five months after Brooke's disappearance, police had a third strong suspect—Aeryn Evans. Evans had been arrested the month before for attacking a Oregon State student on campus. Evans' step sister called police after the incident suspecting that he may have been involved in Wilberger's disappearance too, but this was quickly discovered to be impossible by police.

Frustrated by having to eliminate three great suspects in a row, police decided they needed to take a different approach in the hunt for Wilberger's abductor. They decided to focus in on the one piece of evidence they had directly connected to the person who took Brooke—a green Dodge Caravan.

Police suspected that the green van was connected to Brooke's disappearance because of the two earlier reports from Randy and Crystal on the Oregon State campus, as well as from a tip call from a man who identified himself as Brian. Brian told police that he had seen a green van driving around the area Brooke was last seen. The driver was acting suspicious enough that the van had stood out to the man. The three incidents were too bizarre for police not to connect with Brooke's disappearance on the same day.

Both Randy and Crystal were interviewed by police, but neither were able to give a clear description of the van's driver. They had both been too spooked at the time. However, the coach that had intervened in Crystal's encounter with the van had gotten a good look at the van itself and was able to provide police with more details, including the fact that the van had had Minnesota license plates.

While police were now convinced that the van seen on the Oregon State University was the van used in Wilberger's abduction, they still had no idea where to find the van, and no idea who had been driving it. By November, 2004, six months after Brooke's abduction, investigators assigned to the case were still on square one. Little did they know though, that another crime was about to be committed in Albuquerque, New Mexico, and this crime would lead them right to Wilberger's killer.

Chapter 5

On November 29, 2004, a 22-year-old Russian exchange student, who goes by the pseudonym Natalie Kirov, left the daycare she worked at on the University of New Mexico campus for home. Minutes away from her doorstep, a car pulled up next to her and a man jumped out and told her to get into the car. Terrified, she complied.

The man held Kirov captive in his car at knifepoint as he drove off. When they got to a secluded area of a dead end road, the man pulled the car over and began to sexually assault the young woman, forcing her to remove her clothes in the process.

After sexually assaulting the Russian beauty, the man declared that he needed a drug fix, a "pick-me-up," and drove to a shady apartment complex to purchase some crack. He left Kirov in his car, bound up with her own shoelaces. While her captor was inside, Kirov managed to free her hands and unlock the car. She immediately ran into the street, despite being mostly naked, and flagged down a passing car.

Just as Kirov settles into the car she flagged down her captor emerged from the nearby apartment. After seeing how terrified Kirov became, her saviours quickly drove off in the opposite direction and brought her to the police station. She was finally safe.

Police immediately responded to Kirov's report by visiting the apartments her attacker stopped in to buy his drugs. They were able to find a lady willing to admit that a guy named Joel matching Kirov's description had stopped by earlier that night. Further, she knew where Joel lived.

Police immediately proceeded to the address given to them and immediately spotted the red car Kirov described parked in the lot outside. Police had just begun examining the vehicle when they were approached by a man who said he owned the car. Police asked him if his name was Joel, and he immediately responded yes. Police responded in turn by arresting him.

The Joel police now had in custody was Joel Courtney—a 38-year-old mechanic fisherman. Joel lived in Albuquerque with his wife and three children, but his marriage was incredibly unstable. Only a few weeks before this arrest, Courtney's wife had taken out a restraining order on him.

When police dug deeper into Courtney's past, they discovered that he had a long standing drug problem that they were able to trace back to his childhood in Beaverton, Oregon. Courtney had grown up an average, loving family, but his life began deteriorating after he started using drugs at the tender age of 11. By the age of 14, Courtney began repeatedly molesting his sister and cousins, and by the age of 19, he began experimenting with satanism, and was arrested several times for sexual assaults.

Now, many years later, he was back in custody for the sexual assault of Natalie Kirov, but it had been almost 20 years since he had been committed a crime, something Albuquerque detectives were skeptical of. They wondered if he had victimized any other women who crossed his path over the years, so they contacted authorities in Oregon, Courtney's home state, to ask if there were any unsolved crimes that matched Courtney's modis operandi. Almost immediately, Oregon police mentioned the disappearance of Brooke Wilberger six months ago, hoping to finally provide some answers to Wilberger's family and the surrounding communities.

Chapter 6

After having Joel Courtney brought to their attention, the Brooke Wilberger taskforce in Corvallis, Oregon decided to look further into Courtney's past to see if they could connect him to Wilberger's disappearance. They were quickly rewarded for this decision.

Investigators soon found out that Courtney and his wife had only recently moved to Albuquerque, New Mexico. Before that, the couple moved around Oregon frequently looking for cheap accommodations. At the time of Wilberger's disappearance, the couple were living with relatives in Portland, Oregon, an hour's drive away from Corvallis.

Further, investigators found that Courtney had been working for a janitorial company in Corvallis while he lived in Portland. He drove the company's 1997 green Dodge Caravan with Minnesota license plates to and from work each day.

Courtney's van was the exact van police had been trying to track down for the last several months. Armed with this knowledge, police managed to track down the vehicle, which was immediately brought to Portland to be searched for any forensic evidence that may have survived. Specifically, they were looking for any DNA evidence to compare to known samples of Brooke Wilberger and Joel Courtney himself.

While investigators waited for the DNA results to come back from the lab, they looked into Courtney's whereabouts the day Brooke Wilberger disappeared. They discovered that Joel Courtney had actually been expected in court to face a DUI charge that very day.

Police learned that on this day Courtney apparently made a call from Corvallis saying he would be late for his court time, but he never appeared. Police also learned that the next day, a disheveled Courtney had shown up at a family member's house 16-hours away from Corvallis. When asked why he was in such a state, Courtney came up with a story of how he ran into a gang of men in the woods who had captured a young woman and forced him to do terrible things he did not want to do. Amazingly, the family member chalked the unbelievable story to Courtney's chronic drug use, and never asked about it again.

On the one-year anniversary of Brooke Wilberger's disappearance, Corvallis investigators finally received the results of the forensic sweep of the green Dodge Caravan. It was worth the wait.

The evidence recovered from the van conclusively proved that not only had both Brooke Wilberger and Joel Courtney been in the green van, but Joel Courtney had been the person to place Wilberger there, and he likely knew where she was now. The final challenge investigators now had was getting Courtney to reveal this information so they could finally bring Brooke home.

Chapter 7

On August 2, 2005, Joel Courtney, who is preparing to go on trial for the kidnap and sexual assault of Natalie Kirov is served an arrest warrant for the kidnap and presumptive murder of Brooke Wilberger. Weeks later, the Kirov case is brought to trial, and faced with the indisputable evidence against him, Courtney pleaded guilty. He was given a sentence of 18 years in prison.

But Joel Courtney didn't have long to get settled in the New Mexico prison system. In April of 2008, he was extradited to Oregon in order to stand on trial for the charges laid against him in Brooke Wilberger's case.

When the trial began in Spring of 2009, the prosecutors in the case showed the court Joel Courtney's long standing history of sexual assaults against women, which dated back to his late teen years. They also presented a witness that had seen Courtney the night before Wilberger's abduction. This individual stated that they used to work together, and that they had spent the night of May 23, 2004, drinking and smoking crack together.

Although prosecutors had a large amount of evidence against Courtney, they were missing something very important, something desired not only by them but also by Wilberger's family and the entire community of Corvallis and Eugene—Brooke.

Up to this point, investigators had been unable to find any indication of Brooke's final resting place, and Courtney wasn't about to give this information up easily. The Wilberger family was all but begging the prosecutors and investigators working on Brooke's case to make a deal with Courtney so they could bring their daughter home and give her a peaceful burial.

The District Attorney eventually succumbed to the Wilbergers' wishes and presented a plea deal to Joel Courtney. The terms of the plea deal stated that Courtney needed to plead guilty to all charges against him and reveal the location of Brooke's remains. In exchange, Courtney would receive life in prison without parole.

Courtney rejected this initial offer, but quickly returned to the bargaining table. Courtney offered to plead guilty to the crime if he could be locked up in New Mexico near his family instead of in

Oregon. He also promised to reveal the location of Brooke Wilberger's remains. Courtney's counter-offer was accepted and signed.

To uphold his side of the plea deal, Joel Courtney drew a map to Brooke's burial site for investigators and walked them through the events of May 24, 2004. He told investigators the story of how he forced the young woman into his van and took her to some nearby woods to sexually assault her. After being raped, Wilberger became enraged, and tried to fight her way to freedom. Courtney responded by punching Wilberger until she fell unconscious before beating her to her certain death with a piece of wood he found nearby.

Based on this confession, and armed with Courtney's map, investigators drove 10 miles outside of Corvallis to a heavily wooded area known as the Coast Range. Their goal: to locate Brooke's remains.

After several days of searching, investigators were finally able to locate Brooke Wilberger's remains in a shallow grave next to a clearing of trees. Her grave was hidden beneath a mound of tree branches and leaves. For the Wilbergers, the news was bittersweet. They finally knew what happened to their daughter, and they finally could bring her home, but up until this point they had always maintained hope that when she came home she would still be alive.

Joel Courtney was formally sentenced to life in prison without parole two months later, and was brought back to a New Mexico prison where he prepared to spend the rest of his days. It was the end of a violent sexual predator's freedom, but most importantly, it was the end of the mystery that had plagued Oregon police and Brooke Wilberger's friends and family for years.

Brooke was finally home and at peace, and the world was a little safer now with Joel Courtney now behind bars. This is little solace to those who continue to miss Brooke Wilberger dearly, but having some answers is inarguably better than none. Those who knew Brooke in life remember her as the sweet, caring angel she was. She had a good soul in her heart and a good head on her shoulders and would have undoubtedly achieved great things in life.

Brooke's family still keep in contact with the investigators that dedicated their time to bringing Brooke home—they attend the officers' retirement parties and exchange the occasional email—a small token of the gratitude they will always hold.

MISSING TIFFANY

ANA BENTON

The Disappearance of Tiffany Daniels

As shocking as it might seem, there are over 100,000 missing person cases active in the United States this very second. While the majority of them are eventually found, there is a large percentage of those who have been gone for years. The police extended their investigations as much as they could, and they reached the very end because there was no new information. Finally, those cases simply turn cold.

Missing person cases are particularly difficult for both families and friends. All of them are left without answers about what happened to their loved one, and they are constantly waiting for a break in the case, hoping they will have closure. The Daniels family lived through all of this in the summer of 2013 when their daughter Tiffany went missing one afternoon. It is one of the most perplexing cases in the history of Pensacola, Florida that still puzzles the investigators.

Early life

Tiffany Daniels was born on March 11th, 1988 in Dallas, Texas. She grew up in a loving and supportive family who encouraged her to follow her dreams from an early age. Tiffany loved arts, and that was evident since her high school days. She was very creative and would spend days working on a single painting. Tiffany was not shy at all and had many friends who loved spending time with her because she was always happy and positive.

After finishing high school, Tiffany felt the need to change her scenery so she moved out to Pensacola, Florida. The city had everything Tiffany craved for – long beaches, beautiful nature, and great artistic community. She was an avid hiker and loved spending time in nature. Not to forget that she often went camping on her own just to clear up her mind and relax. Tiffany loved animals, and she was a pescetarian, meaning that her diet didn't contain any meat except for the fish. She also accepted a position at Pensacola State College theater as a set designer. The pay was not spectacular, but Tiffany was doing what she loved, and she could release her artistic side.

Tiffany liked to express herself through dancing as well. It was the perfect way for her to wind down, and she would frequent blues and swing parties downtown. Everyone in those circles knew Tiffany and loved her house gatherings too. Once the dance party comes to an end, Tiffany's friends would get in their vehicles and continue having fun at her home. She was spontaneous, loved the people around her, and enjoyed life to the fullest.

Unfortunately, her caring nature got her into financial problems. Tiffany mostly lived with roommates because she was not able to cover the whole rent herself. However, those roommates would often miss their payments, and Tiffany felt bad for them. She would always pay their share even though she was struggling herself. Unfortunately, those roommates would use her kindness, and they never pay Tiffany back. In the end, Tiffany's bank account was almost empty, and she was looking for a responsible roommate who could actually afford to live with her. She ended up placing a Craigslist ad, hoping she would have more luck with the next roommate.

Gary Nichols who was 54 years old at the time saw the ad and contacted Tiffany since he needed a place to stay as soon as possible. Gary was the father of one of Tiffany's friends, and he was going through a divorce. Even though the difference in age was evident, Tiffany accepted her new roommate with open arms, and the two of them started getting along really well. Gary was financially stable, so Tiffany knew that the rent will not be a problem for him. Additionally, they had similar interests because Gary was very active, and both of them followed the same diet. Gary moved in during July of 2013, and Tiffany hoped that her issues with tenants were over.

Tiffany was in a relationship at the time, and her boyfriend's name was Grey Thomas. They met in the summer of 2012 at a dance party and were inseparable since then. He just got accepted to the graduate program at the University of Texas located in Austin. He decided to move there and urged Tiffany to join him. However, Tiffany was not eager to leave Florida, but she still wanted to have a long-distance relationship with him. The two have made plans for her to visit in a couple of weeks, and Tiffany was happy because it was clear he cared about her as well. Grey hoped Tiffany will like Austin and that she would eventually change her mind about moving there.

The day of the disappearance

Tiffany's boyfriend was supposed to head out to Texas on August 11th, 2013 and the two of them met for a breakfast where they said goodbyes to each other. They will be apart for a couple of weeks and simply had to spend some time together before his trip. Gary Nichols saw Tiffany that afternoon, and he did notice that she was a bit sad about the fact that her boyfriend was leaving which was understandable. But she soon started talking about the trip to Austin she was planning and her mood brightened up immediately.

Since Pensacola State College theater was preparing to start the production of the musical called *Spamalot*, Tiffany had a lot of work ahead of her. *Spamalot* was based on the movie called *Monty Python and the Holy Grail* so Tiffany decided to re-watch it just to get inspired. After all, she was in charge of the set and wanted to do a great job. Gary Nichols was at the house, so he joined her in front of the TV set. The two watched the movie up until midnight and then went to sleep. Both of them had to get up early for work. Sometime around 05:00 AM Gary heard the front door opening and closing several times. He thought it must be Tiffany, but he was a bit confused because he knew that she was not an early riser. As a matter of fact, her job started at 08:00 AM so this was very unusual.

Gary got up and went work at 07:00 AM. The first thing he noticed when he exited the house was that Tiffany's car was gone. He assumed she went to work earlier because it was the first day of *Spamalot* production. Tiffany probably wanted to get more things done. Tiffany's boss did confirm that she showed up for work on schedule but asked him to leave earlier. Tiffany also mentioned that she will not be in town for a couple of days and wanted to inform him about it. Tiffany didn't mention where she was going and didn't provide any additional information. The boss simply concluded that she might have some family business, or wanted to go camping. Tiffany left the theater around 04:45 PM.

Gary came home from work as usual but Tiffany wasn't there. It was strange because she didn't mention she was leaving or anything similar. Tiffany was very responsible and would always tell her friends and family about her plans. Even though Gary was her roommate for a short time, he got to know Tiffany and was sure that she would bring up an upcoming trip. Gary called his daughter Noel who was Tiffany's friend and asked her if she knew anything about Tiffany's whereabouts. She told him not to worry and that Tiffany would show up soon because she was probably staying with friends or working overtime.

The power was cut off the next day, and Gary assumed that Tiffany forgot to pay the bills. He tried contacting her, but nobody answered the cell phone. Worried that something happened to her, he once again urged his daughter Noel to contact Tiffany's mother Cindy and see if she could get a hold of her. Noel sent her a Facebook message, and Tiffany's mother brushed it off because her daughter was a free spirit and had a tendency to go out in nature. Perhaps she had no signal, or she didn't hear the phone ringing. But as the days went on without a single word from Tiffany, everyone started feeling a bit uneasy about the situation.

The search for Tiffany

Tiffany's family got really concerned after they realized that they couldn't reach her for several days. Her cell phone kept ringing, but nobody was answering. Cindy Daniels decided to start calling Tiffany's friends to see if anyone knew where her daughter was. She contacted Noel Nichols, and the two of them made a list of people they should contact. As they went through the list, they realized that no one had seen Tiffany for a week and they all assumed she was staying with another friend. Cindy was really worried, and she contacted the law enforcement to report that her daughter was missing.

Cindy went straight to Escambia County sheriff's office, but the law enforcement didn't take her seriously. They did send out a patrol car to her house to take a statement. The officers thought that since Tiffany was young and free-spirited, she is probably somewhere having a blast and she would turn up soon. But Cindy persisted, and they took a closer look at the case. Escambia County sheriff's office realized that the missing person case was not in their jurisdiction because Tiffany lived in Pensacola and that was also the location she was last seen at. Pensacola Police Department was not dismissive of the report, and they were quickly out on the scene.

Cindy was already at Tiffany's place of residence when the detective Daniel Harnett arrived there to investigate if there was anything suspicious in the house. Tiffany's mother was asked to wait in front of the house. The detective and an officer went through the rooms together and found Tiffany's camping gear. This meant that she wasn't taking a break somewhere in the woods. There were also no signs that she packed her things for any type of trip. Detective Harnett asked Cindy about Tiffany's personal life, focusing on her boyfriend Grey Thomas. Cindy told him that he left for Texas one day before Tiffany's disappearance and this made Detective Harnett focus on the possibility that Tiffany decided to follow him there. However, one of Tiffany's closest friends said: *"Tiffany was a very spontaneous person, but she was also a reliable person. My opinion is if she said that she would be somewhere, she would be there."*

Rodney Daniels, Tiffany's father called Grey Thomas to see if she was there with him. He told him that he spoke to Tiffany on the day of his arrival to Texas, but he hasn't heard from her afterward. Knowing that the majority of disappearances are often followed by a murder, Detective Harnett couldn't rule out the option that Grey returned to Pensacola one day later and hurt Tiffany for some reason. He contacted Grey, asking him to go to his local police station and give them his DNA. They needed to have it in a database in case some new evidence turns up during the investigation. Curious about Grey's whereabouts on the day of the disappearance, Detective Harnett requested Grey's cellphone data. It showed that Grey was in Austin, Texas since the day he left Pensacola.

Running out of reasons for the disappearance, the investigators started interviewing the entire family. They started viewing the case as a possible suicide, so Detective Harnett asked a lot of questions about Tiffany's mental state. Her sister Candace McAdams who lived out of state was very close to Tiffany. The two of them spoke over the phone at least a couple of times every week. Candace mentioned that she noticed a change in Tiffany's behavior sometime in 2012. She was not as happy as she used to be and Candace though that she might be keeping something from her. But nobody could be certain that she was depressed or had any mental problems.

After questioning the neighbors, the investigators found out that Tiffany did come back home after work on the day of her disappearance. Her car was seen briefly in front of the house. Gary Nichols was there at the time, but he didn't see her come in. He was talking with his girlfriend on the phone, and the chances are he was simply too engaged in the conversation to register that someone opened the front door. Cindy thought this was strange because the house itself wasn't large. She stated: *"In Tiffany's room the top of her closet had a foot missing of it. Clear through to the next room. You could throw something through it. I find it hard to believe he couldn't hear her through the room but he heard her going in and out of the house early in the morning."* However, the police dismissed Gary as a suspect because there were no traces of foul play anywhere, and he was the first one to start worrying about Tiffany. Detective Hartnett said: *"Gary seemed appropriate. There was nothing unclear in anything he told us to raise an alarm."*

The discovery of the car

Detective Harnett alerted the media right away about Tiffany's 1999 Toyota 4Runner car, hoping that someone might have seen it somewhere. The TV stations broadcasted the images for days, while Tiffany's friends went around Pensacola, putting up the fliers. And soon enough, the police had their first solid lead. Tiffany's car was spotted at a parking lot at Park West in Pensacola Beach. A jogger who was out running on the morning of August 20th, 2013 thought that the vehicle looked familiar and connected the dots. He also knew the Daniels family, as well as Tiffany herself. Tiffany's mother said: *"I felt something bad happened as soon as they located the car. I believed she was still on the island and that we would find her."*

Once the police arrived, they inspected the abandoned car. It was not too dirty from the outside, and it looked like it was out in the elements for a couple of days. They found Tiffany's bicycle on the inside, alongside her purse, a wallet, a cell phone, a couple of paintings, a jar of peanut butter, and a bottle of water. The forensic team analyzed the car and found two suspicious fingerprints on the car and the steering wheel. After a thorough examination, they determined that the fingerprints didn't belong to Tiffany or any of the officers who were on the scene. Then they proceeded to run them through the database but got no hits.

The parking lot where the car was found was right next to the beach. It was a very popular spot for both locals and tourists. Tiffany's friends and family though that someone must have seen something in the days following the disappearance. The police weren't enthusiastic about it because Tiffany's car was not very distinctive and they were certain nobody would have noticed when it arrived or who was driving it. Not to forget that there were two condominium complexes on the other side of the parking lot. It was summertime and people would usually hang out on their balconies, trying to cool down from the heat.

Tiffany's friends started going around, handing out the flyers, and talking to the people living in the apartment buildings. One resident told them that he was sure the car was not in the parking lot two days ago because he has a good view of it and would have noted if a particular vehicle was parked there for a longer period of time. A couple of people said that they saw a man driving and exiting the car. All of the information was written down and presented to the detectives. They were conducting their own investigation at the time that included toll booths at the Bob Sikes Bridge.

Since Park West was located on Santa Rosa Island, only one bridge connected it to the mainland. The bridge has toll booths, and every vehicle that crosses over is captured by the surveillance cameras. Unfortunately, the cameras monitor the license plates only so finding out who was driving the car was impossible. On the other hand, this information would provide the investigators with the exact time when Tiffany's Toyota crossed the bridge. The detectives went through the images of vehicles that entered Santa Rosa Island on the day Tiffany disappeared and discovered that her car passed the toll booths on August 12th, 2013 at 07:51 PM. This was three hours after she left the theater.

The search of Santa Rosa Island

The detectives, as well as the family, had many theories about what might have happened to Tiffany on Santa Rosa Island. The forensic team determined that the tires of her bike had sand on them which led them to speculate that she went on a ride that night. She might have placed the bike in her car and proceeded to the beach to watch the meteor shower or take a swim in the ocean. The currents are incredibly strong in that area, and she could have been pulled under, unable to swim back to the shore.

Led by this thought, the detectives suspected that her body might appear on the shore of Santa Rosa Island. The island itself was large and searching it would be quite a task. Tiffany's parents found out about KLAAS organization that would gather up the volunteers from the area in order to search for missing children. They contacted the people in charge, and they agreed to help out with the search of Santa Rosa Island. The teams had a lot of grounds to cover, but they had plenty of help from the other search organizations in Florida. They searched the island by foot, going through the entire national park. There was no sign of Tiffany or any items that could be connected to her.

The fact that they didn't find any traces was encouraging to Tiffany's family because this meant that she might be alive somewhere. But it was unlikely that she was still on the island. They needed to widen up the search and let everyone know that Tiffany was missing. Noel Nichols decided to set up a Facebook page in order to help find Tiffany. She uploaded her photos as well as the images of her distinctive foot tattoos. Other users were sharing the information, and soon the tips started coming in.

The sightings

Noel sent every single information she got through the Facebook page to the detective working on this case. Detective Daniel Harnett, eager to find Tiffany, was willing to check every possible sighting. A few weeks after setting up the page, Noel received a tip from a local store. A clerk claimed that Tiffany entered the shop and bought some groceries. He was able to provide a full description of the girl which sparked the interest. Unfortunately, Detective Harnett asked for the surveillance tapes, and Tiffany was not on them. The clerk simply wanted to become a part of the investigation at any cost.

But the next possible sighting gave Tiffany's parents hope that she was out there somewhere. A waitress from Metairie, Louisiana sent a message through Facebook in January of 2014 saying that she might have seen Tiffany a couple of weeks after her disappearance. The woman didn't contact anyone because she was not sure if the girl in the restaurant was indeed Tiffany. However, she couldn't stop thinking about it and decided to let the family know. There was something strange about that encounter, and the waitress thought that it might be important.

She recalls that three women came into the restaurant one night. Two of them were younger, while the third one was significantly older than them. The older woman wore expensive clothes, while the other two did not. They also had long sleeved shirts, which was an odd sight in New Orleans during the summer and autumn. The waitress found it unusual that the older woman was the only one communicating with her. The young women simply sat there in silence, trying not to make an eye contact with the waitress. One of them spoke up to ask if the soups on the menu had fish in them, and the waitress took a good look at her face. It seemed familiar to her and she asked right away if she was the woman who went missing in Florida.

The mood at the table shifted instantly. The whole group got up and left the restaurant. The tip sounded credible because Tiffany was a pescetarian, and she was very concerned about her diet. The family asked if the waitress could provide any surveillance videos that would give them proof that Tiffany was there. She told them that the tapes were long gone because they record over the old footage regularly. While this didn't give the investigators any concrete proof that Tiffany was out there, the tip led Tiffany's family to form another theory – that she was a victim of human trafficking.

White Tiffany didn't fit the profile of a typical human trafficking victim, nothing can be dismissed in this case. There was a possibility that she was kidnapped from the beach and transported to New Orleans soon after her disappearance. Tiffany's family dug deeper and found connections with another incident when a young woman was taken to the same city by two men. She was then forced to become a sex worker. Human trafficking is an ongoing problem in the United States, and the police are doing everything in order to prevent it.

However, they simply cannot save all of the victims right away. Instead, they are familiar with the known human trafficking routes and the local patrol cars often monitor the movement on them. One of the routes is the Interstate 10 that passes through Pensacola. This very fact made Tiffany's parents believe that she met someone on the night of the disappearance and they probably took advantage of her. Tiffany was friendly and loved talking to other people. She might have bumped into someone who seemed trusting but had bad intentions. Unfortunately, the police still had little information, and they were unable to pursue this tip. The case remained open, but there were no new leads.

The revival of the case

The Investigation Discovery channel was aware of the case, and they decided to include it in the new season of their popular show called *Disappeared*. In it, they cover the missing person cases hoping that the media exposure would prompt the possible witnesses to contact the authorities and provide them with new details that could revive the case. Their crew visited Pensacola and talked to almost everyone involved with the investigation, including the lead detective and

Tiffany's parents. The whole city knew that the Investigation Discovery crew was there and people were once again talking about the case.

Four months after they completed the filming, Pensacola Police Department was contacted by a new eyewitness who claimed they had information about the case. The witness told Detective Hartnett that they saw a man opening the trunk of Tiffany's car on the parking lot in Park West. The man was wearing red shorts, and he was in his thirties. This confirmed the statements made by the tenants from the nearby apartment building who claimed that the vehicle was driven by a man. Unfortunately, they weren't able to identify the said individual.

Tiffany Daniels' disappearance is still being investigated, and the authorities are hoping that someone will come forward soon. There has not been a confirmed sighting since August 12th, 2013 but they are not ruling out the possibility that she is alive. The investigators never found her body, so any scenario is possible. The family and friends are managing the Facebook page about Tiffany, and they are updating it regularly, doing their best to keep her in the media. The case remains a true mystery that will hopefully be resolved one day.

THE DISAPPEARANCE OF KELSIE SCHELLING

ANA BENSON

Every time a woman goes missing or is found murdered, the police usually takes a closer look at their spouses or boyfriends. It is a standard procedure, especially if there were indications that they were in a troubled relationship. The disappearance of Kelsie Schelling is one of the biggest mysteries in Colorado. This young pregnant woman was last seen in February of 2013 and the case is still open to this day.

However, Kelsie's family was quite disappointed at the lack of interest by the police to investigate her then-boyfriend Donthe Lucas, who was clearly involved in this crime. After all, Donthe did invite Kelsie to his hometown on that fateful night and he was the last person who saw her alive. When they realized that the police are stalling with the investigation, the family made a promise that Kelsie's case will not be forgotten until they discover what really happened. They kept the public informed through their Facebook page and eventually managed to reach the Colorado Bureau of Investigation.

Early life

Kelsie Jean Schelling was born on 18th February 1991 in Holyoke, Colorado. She grew up in a tightknit family and later became even closer to her mother after the divorce of her parents. Kelsie was only eleven years old when they split up but she would often talk to her father as well. However, they didn't see each other that often because he moved to a different part of town. After graduating from high school, Kelsie attended Northeastern Junior College located in Sterling, Colorado. She was fascinated with psychology and planned to major in it once she gets accepted to the university.

Kelsie was friendly and outspoken, so it comes as no surprise that she had many friends and was a life of every party. During her time at Northeastern Junior College, Kelsie met Donthe Lucas. He was a star player on the basketball team and the two of them fell in love instantly. Donthe Lucas had a very difficult childhood and he grew up in Pueblo, Colorado which is an infamous place known for higher crime rates than anywhere else in the state. He loved basketball and it was clear that he would be an outstanding athlete even in high school. Basketball players do have enormous salaries so Donthe Lucas did see it as an opportunity to help his family out further down the line.

He was hoping that a scout would attend one of his games and recruit him for one of bigger colleges or universities that had a good basketball team. But his big break never happened. Instead, he ended up in Northeastern Junior College which was alright, but Donthe wasn't quite happy with that outcome. His dissatisfaction was evident even in the relationship with Kelsie. Their romance had constant ups and downs, and the two of them would break up, and get back together which drove Kelsie mad. They did finally call it quits after several semesters, and didn't see each other for quite some time.

After finishing the two years at the junior college, Kelsie pursued her education even further, and she moved to California to attend Vanguard University in Costa Mesa. She was finally able to study psychology full time. Donthe continued to play basketball for Emporia State University in Kansas. Kelsie's family was happy she managed to end her relationship with the troubled basketball player, and they hoped that she would make a new life far away from Colorado. Kelsie was independent and she enjoyed living and studying in California. When she wasn't attending classes, Kelsie worked at a tanning salon with her best friend. However, she did drop out of the college because the school work was a bit too much for her at the time and her only option was to go back home. She moved to Denver in 2012 and started working in a store. Meanwhile, Donthe Lucas was back in his hometown Pueblo.

The two of them started talking once again during the autumn of 2012. It was obvious that they still had feelings for each other, so no one was surprised when Donthe and Kelsie decided to spend the Christmas holidays together. The couple seemed happy to everyone around them, but Kelsie did tell her friends that their relationship was still very toxic. Donthe was still treating her badly, calling her names, and starting unnecessary fights. Soon enough everything will change. A few weeks after the holidays, Kelsie found out that she was pregnant. Shocked at first, Kelsie was lost and decided not to tell anyone for a couple of weeks. But keeping a secret was hard. So she called her mother and told her the news. Kelsie's mother Laura would later say that even though her daughter felt a bit stressed, she was still excited about the pregnancy. Yes, she was young but Kelsie was determined to make it work.

Donthe Lucas didn't take the news so well. Having in mind how dissatisfied he felt about his failed basketball career, it is not wrong to assume that the news about a baby simply solidified the fact that his dreams will never come true. Kelsie noticed the change in his mood and openly told him that he doesn't have to be a part of their baby's life. But it is also worth mentioning that Kelsie confided in her best friend that Donthe was ecstatic to become a father at one point. However, his mind was constantly changing. Kelsie went to see her doctor on 4th of February 2013 and he confirmed that she was eight weeks pregnant. The baby was healthy and doing well. The doctor provided her with an ultrasound of the unborn baby, and she was full of joy. Kelsie immediately sent out the pictures to her mother, her friends, and Donthe. Unfortunately, the excitement will not last forever.

The night of the disappearance

Donthe and Kelsey exchanged several emails on February 3rd, 2013. He invited her to visit him in Pueblo. She turned him down saying that she needs to go for a checkup the next day to make sure everything is alright with the baby. After seeing her doctor on the morning of February 4th, 2013, Kelsie went straight to the store. She worked the second shift and was expected to come home sometime after 10:00 PM that night. However, she was in contact with Donthe for the entire day, texting back and forth about the pregnancy. Donthe told her that she should drive out to Pueblo after work because he had a surprise for her. Not knowing what it is, Kelsie asked for more information because Pueblo is two hours away from Denver, and she would probably be tired after work. He insisted that she would be happy with his surprise and that he cannot tell her anything over the phone.

It is safe to assume that Kelsie thought that Donthe was ready to change and start a family with her. Their relationship wasn't a standard one but it seemed like Kelsie was willing to move past all the negative things and focus on the future. So after her shift ended, Kelsie got in her Chevy Cruze LTZ and drove to Pueblo in the middle of the night. Donthe was supposed to meet her in a parking lot in front of a local Walmart. The surveillance cameras did confirm that Kelsie got there on time, but Donthe was nowhere to be seen. She waited in a parked car for almost an hour before sending another text message to Donthe, saying that she has been in the parking lot for too long and that she would come pick him up at whatever location he is at the moment. She got a reply sometime around 12:15 AM.

Donthe told her that he will be waiting for her in the street next to his grandmother's home. Kelsie is seen exiting the parking lot a couple of minutes after she got the message. She clearly did arrive at the second rendezvous spot, but once again Donthe wasn't there. Kelsie sent him another message asking where is he and Donthe replied that he will be there in a minute. This is the last known communication between these two until sometime before 04:00 AM. After going through the phone records, police did discover that Donthe called Kelsie at 03:54 AM but she didn't pick up. The significance of this mysterious phone call will be revealed later. After reviewing the cell tower pings for both phones, the investigators did discover that they were in close proximity to each other.

The search for Kelsie

Kelsie's mother Laura got really worried the next day because she wasn't able to reach her daughter over the phone. She tried calling numerous times but it went straight to the voicemail. The last message she got from her daughter was the ultrasound image of her unborn child, and Laura wasn't sure if something happened to Kelsie after work, or she was ignoring her calls. Laura contacted Kelsie's friends who told her that she went to Pueblo to meet with Donthe. With no word from her daughter, she called Donthe who picked up his phone and told Laura that he had seen Kelsie last night, but that she drove back home in the morning.

Laura was starting to panic, but she did tell Donthe that she would involve the police if she doesn't hear from her daughter soon. Laura and Kelsie were very close and they did tell each other everything, but she suspected that her daughter kept this information from her because she didn't want Laura to know that she was meeting with Donthe. After all, Laura was aware of the nature of their relationship, and his reluctance to accept the baby. Plus, Laura would probably advise Kelsie not to go to Pueblo in the middle of the night.

Laura contacted the local law enforcement and told them that her daughter was missing. Without any solid leads or evidence, they started asking around for Kelsie. Their first step was to take a closer look at Donthe because he claimed that he was the last person to saw Kelsie. She did travel from Denver just to see him. After checking Kelsie's credit card records, they did notice that the card was used hours after Kelsie's last known contact with Donthe. They reviewed the surveillance of the ATM and noticed that Donthe had the card and picked up $400 from Kelsie's account. They weren't sure if Donthe had Kelsie's agreement to use the card, but that was a felony in the state of Colorado, so he was led to the police station for questioning. He had a lot of things to clear up, starting with the timeline of Kelsie's visit to Pueblo.

Donthe's interview

After being picked up by the police, Donthe told his own version of the story. They did see each other that night and talked until early morning hours. Donthe and Kelsie got into a fight and she felt too agitated to drive back home to Denver. She was also very tired from working the second shift. Instead, Kelsie decided to sleep in her car which was parked near his grandmother's house. According to Donthe, his phone rang sometime around 07:00 AM and it was Kelsie. She wasn't feeling well and asked Donthe to drive her to a hospital. He put on his clothes, got to her car, and drove her to the Parkview Hospital.

Kelsie wasn't sure if something happened to the baby during their argument last night and she insisted to see a doctor before she heads out to Denver. Donthe sat inside her car in the parking lot for two hours when she finally emerged from the hospital. Kelsie told him that she had lost the baby. She then asked Donthe to drive her to Walmart to get something to eat and buy some snacks for the road. The two of them started fighting while they were in Walmart and Kelsie refused to drive him home. Donthe simply walked away and got to his grandmother's house on foot. He didn't see Kelsie later in the day and he assumed she went home. He didn't mention stopping at the ATM to pick up the money during his initial interview.

The investigators did notice a couple of possible leads that could collaborate Donthe's story, namely the Parkview Hospital. Each medical facility keeps detailed records of the patients they treat. After speaking to the staff and going through the data, they have confirmed that Kelsie didn't check in during the morning of February 5th. There were also numerous surveillance cameras all over the building and none of them picked up Kelsie entering or leaving the hospital. It was obvious that this part of Donthe's story was not true.

Of course, the police investigators decided to check out Walmart as well because the parking lot and stores do have surveillance cameras, and they might have picked up something that would be of use. While they couldn't find Kelsie or Donthe entering the Walmart, they did notice Kelsie's car on the parking lot. However, the timeline didn't match up with Donthe's story because Kelsie's car appeared at noon, and not in the morning. Plus, Donthe was the only passenger in the car.

Another surveillance camera which was positioned on the back side of Walmart did record Donthe getting into his mother's car – another detail he failed to mention in the initial talk with the investigators.

Without any proof that Donthe's version of the events is true, they called him up for a second interview. The investigators did have a plan this time - they wanted to find out more about the ATM, and how it fits into his timeline. He told the detectives that he took $400 in order to pay his bills and that Kelsie lent him the money since he was at the ATM while Kelsie was at the hospital. When the detectives told Donthe that there is no record of Kelsie ever being in that hospital, his reply was: "I don't even know what to say right now."

They also presented him with Walmart surveillance video that proves Donthe was the only person in the car. He was surprised with the evidence put in front of him, and before the detectives managed to get him to open up, he decided to lawyer up. He was only charged with the identity theft due to the fact that he used Kelsie's credit card, but the case was dropped. The judge had determined that Donthe did use Kelsie's credit card in the past and it was a normal behavior. However, nobody managed to figure out why Donthe had her card in the first place. After all, if Kelsie decided to ran away and start a new life, she would need the money, as well as her vehicle.

Speaking of Kelsie's car, the investigators took a closer look at the surveillance video from Walmart parking lot because they wanted to follow the vehicle. Exactly one day after Donthe left Kelsie's car there, another man approached the car and got inside by using the key. He didn't break in or steal the car. The man was dressed in black, wearing a hoodie, so identifying him was almost impossible. His body type was different than Donthe's, and the mystery man was significantly shorter. Keep in mind that Donthe was a tall basketball player, so his height would be noticeable, even in a low-quality video.

Seeing the direction in which the car went, the police collected the surveillance videos from stores and businesses which were in close proximity. They put the puzzle pieces together and found a route but they couldn't follow it all the way. One day later, the car was dropped at the parking lot of Saint Mary Corwin Hospital. The man locked the car and walked away. The investigators located the vehicle on 14th of February, 2013 and figured out the timeline. But nobody knows where the car was during 6th of February. There weren't any signs of a struggle that would indicate that Kelsie was killed in her car. Almost all of her personal items were missing, including her wallet and a backpack.

While it is unclear if the vehicle was tested for the traces of DNA, an unnamed police officer who worked for Pueblo Police Department will later say that they did find bodily fluids in the trunk of Kelsie's car, as well as two palm prints. However, no one knows what happened with this evidence and was it ever tested. It is simply another thing which the police investigators decided to ignore in this case. Unfortunately, the whole investigation will be under scrutiny soon after.

Theories

Figuring out a solid theory without too many evidence or information can be challenging. Laura, Kelsie's mother, claims that her daughter was probably murdered and that it was premeditated. The first red flag for her was Donthe's initial invitation to meet him before the doctor's appointment. When Kelsie refused, he knew that he had to act fast. Donthe lured Kelsie to Pueblo by saying that he has something to show her, but he never gave an explanation to the law enforcement about what the surprise really was.

It is clear that Kelsie was alive and well up until the point she met Donthe in the street next to his grandmother's house. This is where the trail goes cold. The activity on her phone stops until 04:00 AM. If we analyze the location of the phones, another theory is that Donthe led Kelsie to a remote location and harmed her. It was possible that Kelsie dropped her phone in the middle of a struggle. Donthe couldn't find the phone in the dark, so he had to call her number. He was very likely getting rid of the evidence.

There is a possibility that the two of them did indeed get into a fight, and that an unfortunate accident happened. However, it is more likely that Donthe planned to get rid of Kelsie, and had planned every single step he would take that night. He really insisted to see her as soon as possible. While it is not fair to put the blame on the rest of Lucas family, the fact that his mother picked him up immediately after he left Kelsie's vehicle at the Walmart's parking lot indicates that she knew what was going on. Pueblo Police Department did stop investigating Donthe, and they claimed they didn't have enough physical evidence to prove that a crime really occurred. But they did receive a couple of noteworthy tips which were ignored and never pursued.

The missed opportunities

The entire investigation of the disappearance of Kelsie Schelling was troubling from the very beginning. While the detectives did not have physical evidence of a crime, it was clear that Donthe was the last person who saw Kelsie alive. In every standard investigation, he would have been the prime suspect, and the investigators would do their best to find more proof that he was somehow connected to the crime. The cell tower pings did show that both of their phones were in a remote area next to Pueblo in the early morning hours.

But there are even bigger missed opportunities that could have provided the investigators with the proof they needed. For instance, Donthe was living in his grandmother's house at the time of Kelsie's disappearance. However, the entire family moved out soon after. The landlord started redecorating the house because he wanted to rent it again. He did hear about the missing girl from Denver but had no idea about the details of the case, or the fact that the Lucas family was involved in any way.

He decided to put the new carpets in and when he lifted the old one, the landlord noticed a strange stain on the bottom. He contacted the police enforcement because he was worried that something bad has happened in the house. However, the police ignored his request to check out the stained carpet, and no one had ever arrived at Lucas' previous residence to pick it up. The landlord ended up throwing the carpet away because he simply couldn't keep it forever in the house and wanted to move on with the renovation.

Another missed opportunity involved a couple of fishermen who were out on a lake on a night fishing expedition. It is important to mention that the lake was located near the Saint Mary Corwin Hospital. As you might recall, that was the spot where the police officers discovered Kelsie's vehicle on the 14th of February 2013. They were out on a bank when a hook got stuck to something poking out of the sand. The fishermen went to investigate and were sure that they saw a part of a human ribcage, as well as a skull.

They were terrified by that discovery and left the area right away. Both of them were reluctant to notify the police because they did have some troubles with the law in the past. But that didn't stop them from telling this story to their friends who urged them to contact the local law enforcement. A couple of months passed before they finally talked to the police, but the lake wasn't searched afterward.

The current searches

Family and friends continued to search for Kelsie even after it was clear that the police enforcement forgot about her case. They created a Facebook group that was constantly updated with new information. Pueblo Police Department did go through many changes after Kelsie went missing. The lead investigator was replaced with a new one who was willing to cooperate with the Schelling family. The Schellings did offer a large reward for any new leads that might help them locate their missing daughter. The reward was $100,000 at one point.

This eventually led to false claims and misleading messages such as the one which claimed that Kelsie was still alive, but was placed into a sex traffic ring after a hired hitman decided not to kill her.

Laura Schelling contacted the police and told them about the message. Since the investigators decided to follow every lead possible, they dug deeper and even involved the FBI. Their experts did manage to trace the message back to Russia through the IP address so it was clear that this tip was useless.

The biggest break in the case happened in the spring of 2017 when Colorado Bureau of Investigation finally got the authorization from the local law enforcement to join the search. CBI did determine that the prime suspect should be Donthe Lucas, and they got the warrant to search the area around his previous place of residence. A large number of police officers was seen around that house during April of 2017, and they dug up the parts of the backyard using heavy machinery.

The search has been successful and the officers left the scene carrying bags of evidence. However, they stated that they didn't find any traces of Kelsie's remains. Kelsie's family released the following statement after the search: "The past 2 days have been grueling and emotional, ending with the outcome we did not hope for. Kelsie is still missing. There is no way for me to convey to you all the pain that I feel right now. Sincere, heartfelt thanks goes out to the members of Pueblo PD, CBI and Parks & Rec who worked so hard on this search for Kelsie. This was a physically demanding excavation for them and we witnessed how hard they worked. Despite all the issues we have had in the past, the new leadership over Kelsie's case from PPD and active involvement from CBI is giving us hope that an effective investigation is finally taking place."

The case is still active and the police didn't arrest Donthe. But the positive changes are happening and Kelsie's family is certain that they will find the answers they are looking for now that the investigation is finally moving forward.

FOREVER MISSING: THE DISAPPEARANCE OF NATALEE HOLLOWAY

NATHAN NIXON

Natalee Holloway Disappearance

The tragic story of Natalee Holloway still remains a mystery to this day. The events prior to her disappearance are centered on unreliable witnesses, investigators not following proper procedures, and friends who had left her alone with local patrons. To say that a school trip is never supposed to turn out this way is a monumental understatement. Several theories exist as to what really happened to Natalee. The one, glaring truth of the matter is that Natalee was a beautiful, vibrant young woman who is gone far too soon. Many other facts exist. Witnesses, however, do not.

Natalee Holloway was born in 1986 to David and Elizabeth Holloway in Clinton, Mississippi. Following her parents mutual divorce in 1993, she was raised by her mother alongside her younger brother. Natalee made her life in Alabama when her mother re-married to George Twitty. It was here that she prospered in many organizations, extracurricular activities, and academic niches. Natalee attended Mountain Brook High School in Mountain Brook, Alabama. She was a prominent member in the National Honor Society, was a leader on the school dance team, and competed several sports. Through her hard work, she had earned a full scholarship to attend the University of Alabama, where she enter a pre-med course track and eventually earn her Doctorate. This was all assuming she would make it to the next fall.

Upon graduation, 124 graduating Mountain Brook High School seniors took an "unofficial" school trip to Aruba. Aruba is a Dutch holding in the Caribbean. The group of students arrived in Aruba on May 26, 2005. The trip was scheduled for five days. Oddities of this trip were already apparent. While the trip had 7 chaperones, the students were not expected to be watched every second. The chaperones would meet with the full group of students each night to make sure that everything was okay. To say that these students were taking advantage of this was an understatement. "There was wild partying, lots of drinking, lots of room switching every night," Police Commissioner Gerold Dompig, who headed the investigation from mid-2005 to late 2016, said. "We are aware that the Holiday Inn told them they were absolutely not welcome back next year. Natalee, we know, drank all day every day while there. We have statements that proclaim she started every morning with cocktails. Often times so much drinking that she didn't show up for breakfast on two separate mornings."

Liz Cain and Claire Foreman, two of Holloway's classmates, agreed. "The drinking was excessive. We all were going too far and didn't understand the dangers"

Jodi Bearman organized the class trip. The investigation that would soon follow turned up numerous mistakes and irresponsibility's on the part of organizers and chaperones. The obvious problem was the supervision. How can seven chaperones have control of 124 high school graduates in a foreign place? These students were essentially given the freedom to do whatever they wanted with no punishment. Investigators and parents alike could not believe the lack of supervision and authority displayed by the adults. The punishment that Natalee Holloway would suffer was far greater than anyone could have imagined. However, the fact that this was an avoidable mistake is obvious. Natalee Holloway should never have been allowed to be in this position.

It was May 29, 2005. Natalee had packed her luggage and prepared all of her things to board the flight home the next morning. She had positioned her luggage neatly at the foot of her bed and cleaned up her hotel room accordingly. The 124 graduates had one last night of fun before it was time to head home. This was the last time she would be in her hotel room.

Natalee went out on the town with several of her classmates on night of May 29. Typical of the previous nights, she and her classmates had been heavily drinking and interacting with numerous locals. Natalee had a contagious personality and could always strike up a conversation with anyone. As the night drew on into morning, they arrived at Carlos'n Charlies. This was a well-known bar and dance club in the heart of Aruba. Natalee would last be seen at approximately 1:30 A.M. on May 30, 2005. The story was only just beginning.

Natalee had met up with locals seemingly every night she went out. Striking up conversations, drinking excessively, and trusting strangers was common by several of the graduates that were there. The last glimpse of Natalee would prove to be the beginning of a complicated, international investigation that would prove nearly impossible to solve. She left the club that morning with 17-year-old Joran van der Sloot, 21-year-old Deepak Kalpoe, and 18-year-old Satish Kalpoe. The events that took place after that are largely contested. Through many different testimonies by witnesses and suspects, investigators would check every lead and run into heartbreaking dead ends.

Upon the morning sunrise, the graduates arrived to board the flight home. It was time to start the rest of their lives. All of the graduates arrived without problem except for one: Natalee Holloway. Through irresponsible chaperoning of a class trip and complete disregard for holding the safety of these students paramount above a fun time, an 18-year-old girl was missing. Her hotel room looked untouched from the previous evening. Her luggage safely packed in anticipation of leaving. No signs of movement in the room. Not even a towel had been disturbed. It was frighteningly clear that she had not returned to her room from the previous night's adventures. When the students and chaperones realized what was going on, they immediately notified authorities. Aruban police initiated immediate searches of the island and its surrounding waters. No trace of her was found.

Joran van der Sloot is undoubtedly the most central figure to this case. Van der Sloot was a 17-year-old Dutch honors student who lived in Aruba. At first glance, his baby face and focused eyes would seemingly make him very approachable to anyone. This was, apparently, not the first night that Natalee and Joran had met. In previous nights, they hung out at bars and engaged in behavior not known to most high school students. Over the course of the next several years, Joran would lead investigators and the Holloway family on a wild goose chase that involved changing alibis, secret videos, and fraud. The innocent appearance that Joran van der Sloot displayed was only a disguise for the true monster he would prove to be.

The Kalpoe brothers were Surinamese friends of van der Sloot. Their significance is much less publicized beyond the last sighting of Holloway. Natalee was last seen getting into Deepak Kalpoe's car with both van der Sloot and Satish. This has been confirmed true by both witnesses and suspects in one way or another. There are numerous stories told by van Sloot and other later suspects that bring the Kalpoe's back to the forefront of the case. In such a complicated investigation, Joran van der Sloot, Deepak Kalpoe, and Satish Kalpoe emerged as early suspects.

Action was fast when news reached family of the mysterious disappearance of Natalee. Her mother, Beth Twitty, immediately boarded a private jet with friends and departed for Aruba. Upon arriving in Aruba, the Twittys had started searching for themselves. They located the Holiday Inn and began asking questions. They had obtained footage from the nightclub she was last seen at. To Beth Twittys surprise, the Holiday Inn workers recognized Joran van der

Sloot instantly. He had apparently been a regular in the area. The helpful Holiday Inn employees provided Beth and company with Joran's name and address. Within a mere four hours since arriving at Aruba, the Twittys had already obtained more information than investigators had been able to. The Twittys provided Aruba Police with this information. It appeared that a case was forming around Van der Sloot already. However, the mishandling of the case and poor techniques of the Aruba Police Department were already rearing their ugly head. This case would prove to be a showcase of poor work, bitter disappointment, and investigators being led around by the suspects themselves. The first lead, however, was officially created.

The Twittys and their friends went to the home of Joran van der Sloot. They were accompanied by two Aruban policemen. The fact that Van der Sloot was even allowed to be approached in this manner showed quickly the lack of thought given to the early stages of the investigation. At this early point in the case, the extent of the crime was largely unknown. Hoping for the best, the Twittys only wished to find Natalee safely at the home of Van der Sloot. Joran answered the door and initially denied even knowing who Natalee Holloway was. After being confronted with evidence of their rendezvous that morning, Van der Sloot admitted to being with Natalee. Also present at the house was Deepak Kalpoe, who was driving the vehicle that Natalee had entered in to.

Van der Sloot gave a sketchy story of what had happened after they left the nightclub. He informed the Twittys as well as the two policemen that they had taken Natalee to the California Lighthouse area. This area was near the nightclub, perhaps a few miles drive depending on the route taken. Natalee had been emphatic that she wanted to see sharks. After leaving the nightclub at 1:30 A.M. they went straight to this area to sight see. Van der Sloot informed them that they had returned Natalee to the Holiday Inn hotel where she had been staying at 2:00 A.M. Natalee, who was heavily intoxicated, stumbled exiting the vehicle. The men had offered to help Natalee to her room, however she refused their help and continued toward the entrance. It was at this time, according to Van der Sloot, that she was approached by a tall man wearing all black. Thinking this was a security guard, the men drove off. This, according to Van der Sloot, was the last interaction of any kind with Natalee Holloway that they had. Deepak Kalpoe affirmed the story and agreed with the events.

This is the initial story of the events. The initial investigation is, perhaps, the most ridiculed part in this case. Not only were the men not detained for further extensive questioning, they were completely presumed to be telling the truth. This not only wasted valuable time in finding Natalee, it also allowed suspects to plan their next move. The fact that Van der Sloot and Kalpoe had initially denied even knowing who Natalee Holloway was should have been the first sign of a problem. The second, and more major sign of a problem would come in the investigation of the hotel surveillance footage. While this was obviously looked at during the investigation, this is largely an accepted procedure that is typically done prior to confronting a potential suspect.

The surveillance footage, or lack thereof, was arguably the single biggest setback with this case. The fact that Natalee was not seen in any hotel footage that fateful morning would lend investigators to believe that Van der Sloot and Kalpoe were lying. The hitch in this was that many statements from the case could not even prove that all cameras were functional at the time. The next problem was the fact that not every entrance had a surveillance. This would leave reasonable doubt that Natalee could have been dropped off near one of these entrances that was simply inaccessible to the surveillance footage.

Investigators finally felt as though they had caught the break in the case they needed when a blood stain was found in Deepak Kalpoe's car. Searching the car that was captured on surveillance as the same one that transported Natalee Holloway from the nightclub, police discovered what appeared to be a blood stain. After lab testing and further investigation, not only was this not Natalee Holloway's blood, it could not even be proven to be blood at all. Another door was closed in the initial investigation of Natalee's disappearance.

After the first full day of investigation, United States involvement in the case began. Monetary assistance was given immediately to aid the Aruban Police Department. Additionally, American searchers sought to help with the advanced search of coastline that had been a constant since Natalee Holloway missed her flight. United States Secretary of State Condoleezza Rice stated "we are in constant contact with Aruban Police. The safe return of Natalee Holloway continues to be our priority."

Hours after missing her flight, the media's involvement in the case was tremendous. All of the major news stations in the United States began their initial coverage of the story. With little facts to go on, it was largely reported as a missing person case with no evidence of foul play. No suspects had truly been pinpointed at this point. The news of her last being seen in the early hours leaving a nightclub led several to assume the worst from the get go, however. It would not be long before Joran van der Sloot was at the fore front of the investigation as well as the ensuing media storm.

It was just six days after Holloway's disappearance that authorities made their first arrest in the case. On June 5, 2005, Abraham Jones and Nick John were placed under arrest. To this day, the exact reasoning behind their arrest is unknown. One of the men had previous encounters with the law, while both were suspected of previously pacing hotels to pick up women. Both men were security guards at a nearby hotel, the Allegro Hotel. It is likely that the statements made by Van der Sloot and Kalpoe led police to this arrest. The men were released on June 13 with no charges being placed. This is yet another example of flawed work by the investigation. It was obvious that police were trusting of Joran van der Sloot and Deepak Kalpoe from the onset. This is a largely debated topic to this day. Many wonder why Van der Sloot and Kalpoe were not arrested initially. However, this was just scratching the surface of what was to come.

On June 9, Joran van der Sloot and both Kalpoe brothers were arrested on suspicion of the kidnapping and murder of Natalee Holloway. In hindsight, it is absolutely unfathomable that it took investigators 10 days to make these arrest. The only evidence they really had at this point was surveillance of Natalee last being seen with these men. Aruban police reported that these men were the "prime suspects from the get-go." While this may have been true to a point, police waited until June 6 to start extended surveillance of the men. Investigators knew they would need much more evidence than a video of Natalee entering a car with the men from the nightclub. Aruban Police instigated phone taps, video surveillance, tailing their vehicles, and monitoring of their e-mails. At this point, in order to continue to hold the three suspects in custody, they would need to provide increasingly substantial evidence at different check points of the investigation. With increasingly consistent pressure from Natalee Holloway's family, police decided to stop the surveillance activities prematurely and execute the arrest on the men.

The arrest of these three suspects was met with heavy interest from people all over the world. The procedures by police and the heavy involvement of the Holloway family seemingly left everyone with an opinion on what should have been conducted differently. Many media outlets focused on the timing of the surveillance activities. Having taken nearly a week to begin the activities from the time of Natalee's last sighting, many felt it was already too late to incriminate the suspects. Also, the fact that surveillance started at the time they had already arrested Adams and John was a bit odd for normal investigative procedure. Lastly, many assumed that if investigators pursued an arrest after just a few days of surveillance of the men, they must have captured something indisputable to implicate one or all of the suspects. This was simply not the case. Aruban Police had missed the initial window of the investigation. Many critics argue that in the interest of uncovering the truth, an extended surveillance would be necessary for the time period they had waited to begin. Investigators instead buckled to pressure from an unorthodox family interaction in a complicated case.

June 11 was the first of many highly publicized false leads. Aruban Minister of Justice David Cruz indicated, in a statement, that Natalee Holloway was dead and that authorities knew the exact location of her body. This was all over most any major media outlet as an early morning breaking news story. The United States was gripped with curiosity and heartbreak as it seemed the terrible truth had come to fruition. Hours later, Cruz released a follow up statement that they had been the victim of "misinformation." This simply is unacceptable. As an investigator or someone in a position as high as Cruz was, you can't put the wagon before the horse, especially to national media outlets. What was the source of this misinformation? Lead investigator Gerold Dompig reported to the Associated Press that one of the detained men had informed them that "something terrible and unthinkable" had happened on the beach after they left the nightclub. The suspect, it was reported, was leading them to the location of the body. This, of course, was another folly.

On June 16, yet another suspect, Steve Gregory Croes, was arrested. "Croes was detained based on urgent information given to us by one of the other three suspect," Aruban Police Superintendent Jan van der Straaten informed the media. While this arrest didn't yield much as far as new leads, it did start to give the appearance that investigators were at a standstill with the case. Six days later on June 22, Joran van der Sloot's father, Paulus, was arrested. This was largely believed to be a bargaining chip to use against Joran. While Paulus was not a suspect, as later revealed by police, he was interrogated in an effort to get more information on Joran. Both Croes and Paulus van der Sloot were released on June 26.

It was around this time where public opinion began to focus on Joran van der Sloot. It was quite clear to all involved that Van der Sloot was not being truthful in his story. The events made little sense to the general public. The longer that Natalee remained missing, the more likely it was that she was, indeed, dead. The suspicion on Joran would only intensify in the coming day.

From the time of the arrest of Joran van der Sloot and the Kalpoe brothers, their stories changed numerous times. In particular, Van der Sloot was giving three completely conflicting stories that would put the focus solely on him.

The first story shift came, oddly enough, from all three suspects. Van der Sloot and both Kalpoe brothers all agreed that Joran and Natalee had been dropped off at the Marriott Hotel beach near several fisherman huts. Van der Sloot was emphatic that he didn't harm Natalee Holloway in any way. He told investigators that they were both heavily intoxicated, and eventually Natalee passed out on the beach. When this happened, he began to walk home. It was at this time that he made a phone call to Deepak Kalpoe that he was walking home. Van der Sloot claims to have sent Kalpoe a text message 40 minutes later. Oddly enough, the phone call nor text message was found in Van der Sloot's phone records.

Lead investigator Gerold Dompig gave insight into the third different story by the suspects. This story, told by Joran van der Sloot, was a turning point in that it showed that he was willing to change his story however he saw fit in order to avoid suspicion.

"The latest story came when Joran saw that his buddies, the Kalpoe's, were essentially pointing the finger in his direction. He wanted to screw them by pointing the finger right back at them. But the story simply doesn't check out. He just wanted to screw Deepak. They (Deepak and Joran) had great arguments about this in front of the judge. Their stories didn't match. Joran felt the focus shifting to him and was willing to do anything to change it. That girl, she was from

Alabama. She is not going to stay in the car with two black kids while Joran simply gets out of the car to head home alone. We firmly believe the second story; that they were dropped off at the Marriott. This goes along with the timeline and the stories given by the Kalpoe's."

Upon hearings in front of the judge on July 4, both Satish and Deepak Kalpoe were released from custody. Joran van der Sloot was to remain for a minimum of 60 days. Focus was solely on Van der Sloot as the main suspect in the disappearance of Natalee Holloway.

For nearly all of July, searches for Natalee Holloway remained fruitless endeavors. Investigators had no leads and were consistently getting varied stories from Joran van der Sloot. While police had solid suspicions of Van der Sloot, they had essentially zero solid evidence against him. The media storm updated the world daily on search efforts. With each passing day, reality began to set in for many that Natalee Holloway may never be found. Initially, a $50,000 reward was offered for Natalee's safe return. On July 25, the reward for the safe return of Holloway had increased all the way to $1,000,000. In addition, a $100,000 reward was offered for information that would lead to the location of her remains. In August of the same year, the reward for the location of her remains would raise all the way to $250,000. This was widely covered by the media and many local and national governments. This was a final attempt by investigators to break the cold case open. This strategy had several negative impacts, however. The most severe of these were the wasted time on false leads and folly calls. This was not anticipated by investigators as it should have been.

Between July 27 and 30, investigators initiated a massive undertaking. The pond in front of the Aruba Racquet Club was completely drained. This was within one mile of the Marriott Hotel where Van der Sloot had apparently taken Natalee Holloway. A tip was given to police that was especially unique. A gardener had apparently seen Joran van der Sloot driving into the Racquet Club with the Kalpoe brothers. Van der Sloot was said to have been hiding his face. The gardener informed police that the men were seen driving in between 2:30 A.M. and 3:00 A.M. on the morning of May 30. The search of the pond bed and surrounding area, however, yielded no clues.

On July 28, a jogger came forward with a frightening testimony. The United States media covered this story heavily for several days as it was the first story of someone seeing a woman resembling Natalee Holloway since her disappearance. The jogger claimed that she saw a group of men burying a young, blonde haired woman on the afternoon of May 30 at a landfill. The landfill was subsequently searched three separate times with precision. This search, again, yielded no results.

In late August, Joran van der Sloot became the front page villain to many. Throughout the entire case, it was well covered as to how many variations of a story Joran had given. While showing no remorse or empathy for the Holloway family, the public formed a very negative opinion of Van der Sloot. Anita van der Sloot would provide more material for the family. "It's a desperate attempt to get the boys to talk. But there is nothing to talk about. Joran has no fault in this mystery." Joran van der Sloot's mother made this statement after police again brought in the Kalpoe's for questioning. This left a bitter taste in the mouths of many. It was shaping up to be Van der Sloot's versus investigators.

On September 3, 2005, Joran van der Sloot was released from custody due to insufficient evidence to hold. By September 14, all restrictions were officially lifted from Van der Sloot. Whatever the events of May 30, no suspect was in custody and there were no leads for police. Joran van der Sloot was a free man. The release of Van der Sloot created a frenzy among the general public. People all over the United States and surrounding areas were furious, set in their beliefs that a guilty man was walking away free. The nation was gripped against a common villain.

The months that followed Joran van der Sloot's release provided media cannon fodder of epic proportions. Van der Sloot did several interviews and even composed a book of his take on the events of the night. To the public's astonishment, this man was now profiting off of this whole fire storm of a case. The most notable post release interview came with Fox News on a three night special. Van der Sloot claims that the two were heavily intoxicated on the beach after leaving the nightclub. He went into great detail about the two planning an escapade on the beach, narcotic use, and partying in a fun filled night in Aruba. He showed little empathy or remorse for any of the events. He seemingly talked about Natalee as if she was the villain. Joran went on to explain that Natalee wanted to have sex on the beach, however he didn't have a condom. He left her on the beach and was driven home by Satish Kalpoe. Later, Satish Kalpoe's lawyer claims that Satish was asleep well before this would have happened. Joran went on to explain that he was embarrassed for having left a beautiful woman alone on the beach, citing this as the reason for his ever changing story. He said that he was convinced Holloway would turn up.

This all sat so negatively to viewers. There was outrage over the handling of the investigation. People could not understand how no evidence existed to implicate a man that was deemed the perpetrator. Aruba authorities later claimed that over $3 million had been spent on the investigation. This was over 40% of the overall budget for investigative expenditures.

On December 18, 2007 after extensive efforts to implicate the Kalpoe brothers and/or Joran van der Sloot, the case was officially closed. Prosecutors cited lack of evidence to a violent crime, lack of evidence to a murder, as well as lack of continued funding for the expensive investigation. Over two full years after the disappearance of Natalee Holloway, the case was closed. The remains of Natalee Holloway had not been found. Joran van der Sloot not only was a free man, but had profited greatly from the publicity of the case. This, however, would not be the final chapter to the journey of Joran van der Sloot.

In the years after the closing of the Natalee Holloway case, Joran van der Sloot told several variations of events of that fateful morning. He gave countless interviews, seemingly telling a different story in each one of them. Ultimately, Joran van der Sloot was seeking money and fame through his disgusting actions. In an interview with Fox News in 2008, he claimed to have sold Natalee Holloway in sexual slavery. He later retracted the statements in the days after. It was reported in 2010 that in a 2009 interview with RTL group, he claimed he disposed of the body in a marsh area in Aruba. This interview was never confirmed, nor denied by investigators or Van der Sloot.

Remarkably, Van der Sloot would show his greed had no limits. On March 29, 2010 Van der Sloot contacted Beth Twittys legal representative. He offered to give the location to Natalee Holloway's remains in exchange for $25,000. After contacting police, the transaction was made. $15,000 was wired to Van der Sloot's account, and the remaining $10,000 was given by a middle man. The receipt of the transaction was videotaped by police. The information provided by Van der Sloot was proven false, as the building that he claimed housed the remains was not yet built at the time of the disappearance. Van der Sloot would be indicted on June 30 of the same year. However, he was about to be indicted for a much more serious crime.

On May 30, 2010, exactly five years from the time of the disappearance of Natalee Holloway, Stephany Flores Ramirez was reported missing in Lima, Peru. Ironically, she was found dead just three days later in a hotel room registered to Joran van der Sloot. On June 7, 2010, Van der Sloot confessed to killing Ramirez after he lost his temper while she was using his laptop. Within the same interview, he said that he knew where Holloway's body was. Dealing with jurisdiction issues, Peruvian police could not further investigate the Holloway statement without Aruban authorities.

Aruban authorities were granted interrogation of Van der Sloot in Peru in June of 2010. While he would not confess to murdering

Holloway or her whereabouts, he did admit to the extortion plot on the Holloway family. "I wanted to get back at Natalee's family. They have been making my life miserable for the last five years," Van der Sloot said. Van der Sloot was found guilty in the murder of Stephany Flores Ramirez and sentenced to 28 years in prison. This sentence also included his time for his extortion of the Holloway family.

Natalee Holloway's remains have never been found. There have never been any convictions made into the disappearance of Natalee or any criminal wrong doing. In this case, it would be naïve to imagine a scenario where Joran van der Sloot was not responsible in some way for the death of Natalee Holloway. While Van der Sloot waste the best years of his life behind bars, a young woman with an extremely bright future is still gone. Closure will never be possible for the Holloway family. Perhaps a poor investigative strategy is to blame for the lack of any convictions. Maybe it is the irresponsible planning of school personnel and behavior supervision by chaperones could have prevented this tragedy. Better decision by Natalee herself may have helped avoid such a terrible event. In any case, an intelligent young woman who had everything in front of her did not deserve this end. The Holloway family did not deserve this. We will likely never know the true events of that fateful May morning. What we do know is that we will never get to see the true potential that Natalee Holloway had.